Fodor's 98
Pocket Paris

Reprinted from *Fodor's Paris '98*

Fodor's Travel Publications, Inc.
New York • Toronto • London • Sydney • Auckland
www.fodors.com/

Fodor's Pocket Paris '98

EDITORS: Natasha Lesser, Jennifer J. Paull

Editorial Contributors: Robert Andrews, Roberta Beardsley, David Brown, K. Neil Cukier, Christina Knight, Simon Hewitt, Suzanne Rowan Kelleher, Alexander Lobrano, Heidi Sarna, Helayne Schiff, M. T. Schwartzman (Gold Guide editor), Dinah Spritzer

Editorial Production: Laura M. Kidder

Maps: David Lindroth, *cartographer;* Bob Blake, *map editor*

Design: Fabrizio La Rocca, *creative director;* Lyndell Brookhouse-Gil, *cover design;* Jolie Novak, *photo editor*

Production/Manufacturing: Mike Costa

Cover Photograph: Bob Krist/Corbis

Copyright

ISBN 0–679–03523–0

Special Sales

Fodor's Travel Publications are available at special discounts for bulk purchases for sales promotions or premiums. Special editions, including personalized covers, excerpts of existing guides, and corporate imprints, can be created in large quantities for special needs. For more information, contact your local bookseller or write to Special Markets, Fodor's Travel Publications, 201 East 50th Street, New York, NY 10022. Inquiries from Canada should be directed to your local Canadian bookseller or sent to Random House of Canada, Ltd., Marketing Department, 1265 Aerowood Drive, Mississauga, Ontario L4W 1B9. Inquiries from the United Kingdom should be sent to Fodor's Travel Publications, 20 Vauxhall Bridge Road, London SW1V 2SA, England.

PRINTED IN THE UNITED STATES OF AMERICA

10 9 8 7 6 5 4 3 2 1

CONTENTS

Maps

ON THE ROAD WITH FODOR'S

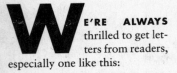**E'RE ALWAYS**
thrilled to get let-
ters from readers,
especially one like this:

It took us an hour to decide what book to buy and we now know we picked the best one. Your book was wonderful, easy to follow, very accurate, and good on point-ing out eating places, informal as well as formal. When we saw other people using your book, we would look at each other and smile.

Our editors and writers are com-mitted to making every Fodor's guide "the best one"—not only accurate but always charming, brimming with sound recommen-dations and ideas, right on the mark in describing restaurants and hotels, and full of facts that make you view what you've traveled to see in a rich new light.

New This Year

Since Paris is a city for wandering, Simon Hewitt has arranged the neighborhoods in a new way, cov-ering more parts of Paris than ever before. Chapter 3 now ends with a list of the best cafés, and a rundown on fantastic shopping neighbor-hoods has been added to Chapter 6. Alexander Lobrano and Suzanne Rowan Kelleher have introduced new hotels and restaurants.

We're also proud to announce that the American Society of Travel Agents has endorsed Fodor's as its guidebook of choice. ASTA is the world's largest and most influen-tial travel trade association, oper-ating in more than 170 countries, with 27,000 members pledged to adhere to a strict code of ethics reflecting the Society's motto, "In-tegrity in Travel." ASTA shares Fodor's devotion to providing smart, honest travel information and advice to travelers, and we've long recommended that our read-ers consult ASTA member agents for the experience and profes-sionalism they bring to the table.

On the Web, check out Fodor's site (www.fodors.com/) for infor-mation on major destinations around the world and travel-savvy interactive features. The Web site also lists 85-plus radio stations na-tionwide that carry the *Fodor's Travel Show*, a live call-in program that airs every weekend. Tune in to hear guests discuss their adven-tures, or call in for answers to your most pressing travel questions.

How to Use This Book

Organization

Up front is **Essential Information**, which is divided alphabetically by topic. Under each listing you'll find tips and information that will help you accomplish what you need to in Paris. You'll also find addresses and telephone numbers of organizations and companies that offer destination-related services.

The first chapter, **Destination: Paris,** helps get you in the mood with a wonderful, evocative essay.

The **Exploring chapter** is divided by neighborhood; each section describes the area's highlights, and then lists sights alphabetically. The **remaining chapters** are arranged alphabetically by subject (dining, lodging, nightlife and the arts, and shopping).

Icons and Symbols

★ Our special recommendations

✕ Restaurant

🏨 Lodging establishment

😋 Good for kids (rubber duckie)

☞ Sends you to another section of the guide for more information

✉ Address

☎ Telephone number

FAX Fax number

☉ Opening and closing times

💰 Admission prices (those we give apply to adults; reduced fees are almost always available for children, students, and senior citizens)

Credit Cards

The following abbreviations are used: **AE,** American Express; **DC,** Diners Club; **MC,** MasterCard; and **V,** Visa.

Please Write to Us

You can use this book in the confidence that prices and opening times are based on information supplied to us at press time; Fodor's cannot accept responsibility for any errors. Time brings changes, so always confirm information. Also, when making reservations be sure to mention if you have a disability or are traveling with children, if you prefer a private bath or a certain type of bed, or if you have specific dietary needs or other concerns.

Were the restaurants we recommended as described? Did our hotel picks exceed your expectations? If you have complaints, we'll look into them and revise our entries when the facts warrant it. So send us your feedback, positive *and* negative: E-mail us at editors@fodors.com (specifying the name of the book on the subject line) or write the Paris editor at Fodor's, 201 East 50th Street, New York, NY 10022. Have a wonderful trip!

Karen Cure

Karen Cure
Editorial Director

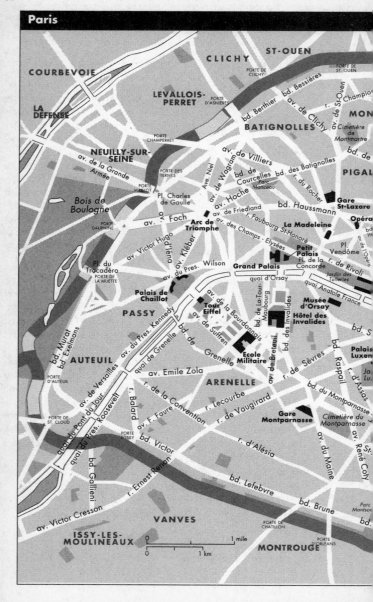

Paris

CLICHY ST-OUEN

COURBEVOIE

PORTE DE CLICHY

PORTE DE ST-OUEN

bd. Berthier

av. de Clichy

r. de St-Ouen

à Champion

LEVALLOIS-PERRET

bd. Bessières

LA DÉFENSE

PORTE D'ASNIÈRES

MON

BATIGNOLLES

Cimetière de Montmartre

PORTE CHAMPERRET

av. de Villiers

bd. de

NEUILLY-SUR-SEINE

PIGAL

av. de la Grande Armée

Ave. Niel

av. de Wagram

bd. de Courcelles

bd. des Batignolles

r. du Rocher

PORTE DES TERNES

Parc Monceau

Gare St-Lazare

PORTE MAILLOT

Pl. Charles de Gaulle

av. Hoche

bd. Haussmann

Bois de Boulogne

av. de Friedland

La Madeleine

Opéra

PORTE DAUPHINE

av. Foch

Arc de Triomphe

av. des Champs - Elysées

r. Faubourg St-Honoré

Petit Palais

Pl. Vendôme

av. de l'Opéra

av. Victor Hugo

r. d'Iéna

av. Kléber

av. du Pres. Wilson

Grand Palais

Pl. de la Concorde

r. de Rivoli

Pl. du Trocadéro

quai d'Orsay

Jardin des Tuileries

quai Anatole France

PORTE DE LA MUETTE

Palais de Chaillot

Tour Eiffel

av. de la Bourdonnais

av. de la Tour-Maubourg

Musée d'Orsay

PASSY

av. de Suffren

Hôtel des Invalides

bd. S

bd. Murat

av. du Pres. Kennedy

bd. de Grenelle

bd. des Invalides

AUTEUIL

bd. Exelmans

quai de Grenelle

Grenelle

Ecole Militaire

av. de Breteuil

r. de Sèvres

Palais Luxen

bd. Raspail

PORTE D'AUTEUIL

av. Emile Zola

ARENELLE

r. d'Assas

Ja Lu.

av. de Versailles

r. de la Convention

r. Lecourbe

r. de Vaugirard

bd. du Montparnasse

PORTE DE ST. CLOUD

qual du Pont du Jour

r. Balard

r. F. Faure

Gare Montparnasse

Cimetière du Montparnasse

quai du Pres. Roosevelt

PORTE D'ISSY

bd. Victor

r. d'Alésia

av. du Maine

St-René Coty

bd. Gallieni

r. Ernest Renan

bd. Lefebvre

Parc Montsou

av. Victor Cresson

VANVES

PORTE DE CHATILLON

bd. Brune

bd.

ISSY-LES-MOULINEAUX

0   1 mile

0   1 km

MONTROUGE

PORTE D'ORLEANS

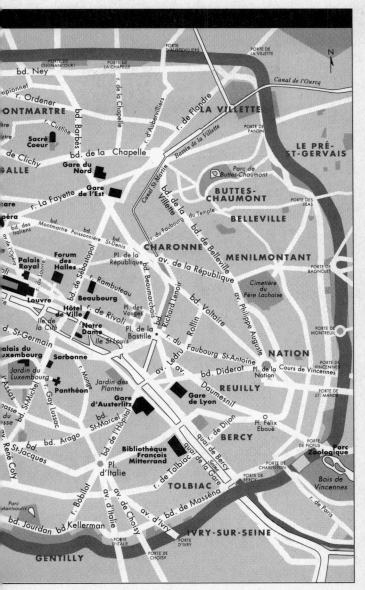

Paris with Arrondissements

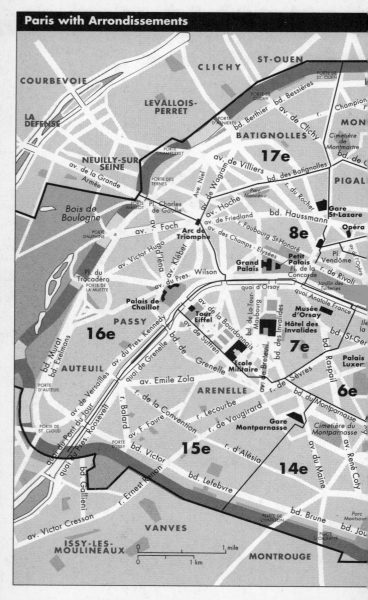

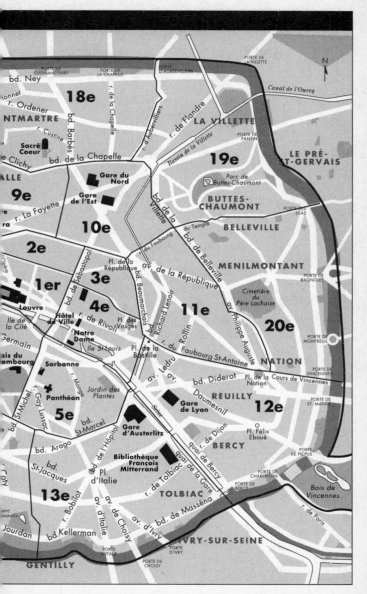

Paris Métro

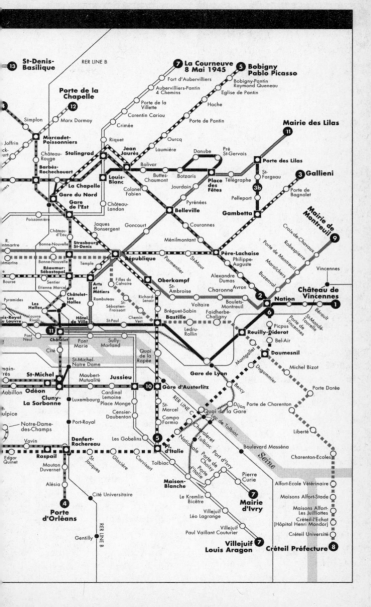

ESSENTIAL INFORMATION

Basic Information on Traveling in Paris, Savvy Tips to Make Your Trip a Breeze, and Companies and Organizations to Contact

AIR TRAVEL

The major airports are **Orly** and **Charles de Gaulle.**

Flying time is 7 hours from New York, 9½ hours from Chicago, and 11 hours from Los Angeles.

AIRPORT INFORMATION➤ Orly (☎ 01/4975–1515). Charles de Gaulle (☎ 01/4862–1212).

CARRIERS

MAJOR AIRLINES➤ **Air France** (☎ 800/237–2747) to Charles de Gaulle. **American Airlines** (☎ 800/433–7300) to Charles de Gaulle, Orly. **Continental** (☎ 800/231–0856) to Charles de Gaulle. **Delta** (☎ 800/241–4141) to Charles de Gaulle. **Northwest** (☎ 800/225–2525) to Charles de Gaulle. **TWA** (☎ 800/892–4141) to Charles de Gaulle. **United** (☎ 800/538–2929) to Charles de Gaulle. **US Airways** (☎ 800/428–4322) to Charles de Gaulle.

FROM THE U.K.➤ **Air France** (☎ 0181/742–6600). **Air U.K.** (☎ 0345/666–777). **British Airways** (☎ 0345/222–111). **British Midland** (☎ 0181/754–7321 or 0345/554–554). All airlines service Charles de Gaulle; British Airways also has flights to Orly.

TRANSFERS

Although rush-hour traffic can make trips from the airports to the city slow and frustrating, you will not be frustrated by a lack of transportation options.

From the Charles de Gaulle airport, **the easiest way to get into Paris is on the RER-B line,** the suburban express train. A station was opened right beneath Terminal 2 in 1994. Trains to central Paris (Les Halles, St-Michel, Luxembourg) leave every 15 minutes. The fare (including métro connection) is 45 francs, and journey time is about 35 minutes. Air France operates a convenient, pleasant bus service to the city. Buses run every 15 minutes between Charles de Gaulle airport and the Arc de Triomphe, with a stop at the Air France air terminal at Porte Maillot, or directly to Montparnasse. The fare is 55 francs, and journey time is about 40 minutes. The Roissybus, operated by the Paris Transit Authority, has buses every 15 minutes to rue Scribe at the Opéra; the cost is 40 francs.

Taxis are readily available. Journey time is around 30 minutes, depending on the traffic, and the fare is between 150 and 200 francs. For substantially less, there is also Paris Airports Service (☞ Shuttle Service *below*), which can provide a private car to meet you on arrival at either Paris airport and drive you to your destination.

The most economical way to reach Paris from Orly by train to take the free shuttle bus from the terminal to the train station, where you pick up a suburban express train on the RER-C line. Trains to Paris leave every 15 minutes. The fare is 28 francs, and journey time is about 35 minutes. You could also take the new monorail service, Orlyval, which runs between the Antony RER-B station and Orly airport every 7 minutes. The fare to downtown Paris is 54 francs. Air France buses run every 12 minutes between Orly airport and the Air France air terminal at Les Invalides on the Left Bank. The fare is 40 francs, and journey time is between 30 and 45 minutes, depending on traffic. The Paris Transit Authority's Orlybus leaves every 15 minutes for the Denfert-Rochereau métro station; cost is 30 francs. Taxis take around 25 minutes in light traffic; the fare will be about 160 francs.

SHUTTLE SERVICE➤ **Paris Airports Service** (☎ 01–49–62–78–78) will pick you up at either Paris airport and drive you directly to your destination. For two or more people, the cost of this service is about the same as a regular taxi fare. You must make reservations two or three days in advance; MasterCard and Visa are accepted.

BUS TRAVEL

For information on bus travel within Paris, *see* Public Transportation, *below*.

FROM THE U.K.

Eurolines (✉ 52 Grosvenor Gardens, London SW1W 0AU, ☎ 0171/730–0202) operates a nightly service from London's Victoria Coach Station, via the Dover–Calais ferry, to Paris. Departures are at 9 AM, arriving at 6 PM; noon, arriving at 9 PM; and 10 PM, arriving at 7 AM. Fares are £60 round-trip (under-25 youth pass £56), £35 one-way. **Hoverspeed** (✉ International Hoverport, Marine Parade, Dover CT17 9TG, ☎ 01304/240241) offers up to four daily departures from Victoria Coach Station. Fares are £60 round-trip, £38 one-way. Make reservations in person at any **National Express** office or at the **Coach Travel Centre** (✉ 13 Regent St., London SW1 4LR). Call to make credit-card reservations (☎ 0171/824–8657).

CAR RENTAL

Before renting a car, consider this: Unless you plan to travel extensively outside the city, a car in Paris is often more of a liability than an asset and parking is extremely difficult.

Rates in Paris begin at $60 a day and $196 a week for an economy car with air-conditioning, a manual transmission, and unlimited mileage. This does not include tax on car rentals, which is 20.6%.

MAJOR AGENCIES➤ **Budget** (☎ 800/527–0700, 0800/181181 in the U.K.). **Dollar** (☎ 800/800–4000; 0990/565656 in the U.K., where it is known as Eurodollar). **Hertz** (☎ 800/654–3001, 800/263–0600 in Canada, 0345/555888 in the U.K.). **National InterRent** (☎ 800/227–3876; 0345/222525 in the U.K., where it is known as Europcar InterRent).

RENTAL WHOLESALERS➤ **Auto Europe** (☎ 207/842–2000 or 800/223–5555, FAX 800–235–6321). **Europe by Car** (☎ 212/581–3040 or 800/223–1516, FAX 212/246–1458). **DER Travel Services** (✉ 9501 W. Devon Ave., Rosemont, IL 60018, ☎ 800/782–2424, FAX 800/282–7474 for information or 800/860–9944 for brochures). The **Kemwel Group** (☎ 914/835–5555 or 800/678–0678, FAX 914/835–5126).

MEET THE REQUIREMENTS
In France your own driver's license is acceptable. An International Driver's Permit is a good idea; it's available from the American or Canadian automobile association, or, in the United Kingdom, from the Automobile Association or Royal Automobile Club.

THE CHANNEL TUNNEL

Short of flying, the Chunnel is the fastest way to cross the English Channel: 35 minutes from Folkestone to Calais, 60 minutes from motorway to motorway, or 3 hours from London's Waterloo Station to Paris's Gare du Nord.

CAR TRANSPORT➤ **Le Shuttle** (☎ 0990/353535 in the U.K.).

PASSENGER SERVICE➤ In the U.K., **Eurostar** (☎ 0345/881881), **InterCity Europe** (✉ Victoria Station, London, ☎ 0990/848848). In the U.S., **BritRail Travel** (☎ 800/677–8585 or 212/575-2667), **Rail Europe** (☎ 800/942–4866).

CUSTOMS & DUTIES

When shopping, **keep receipts** for all of your purchases. Upon re-entering the country, **be ready to show customs officials what you've bought.** If you feel a duty is incorrect, appeal the assessment. If you object to the way your clearance was handled, get the inspector's badge number. In either case, first ask to see a supervisor, then write to the port director at the address listed on your receipt. Send a copy of the receipt and other appropriate documentation. If you still don't get satisfaction you can take your case to customs headquarters in Washington.

ENTERING FRANCE

From outside the European Union (EU), you may import duty free: (1) 200 cigarettes or 100 cigarillos or 50 cigars or 250 grams of tobacco (twice that if you live outside Europe); (2) 2 liters of wine and, in addition, (a) 1 liter of alcohol over 22% volume (most spirits) or (b) 2 liters of alcohol under 22% volume (fortified or sparkling wine) or (c) 2 more liters of table wine; (3) 50 milliliters of perfume and 250 milliliters of toilet water; (4) 200 grams of coffee, 100 grams of tea; and (5) other goods to the value of 300 francs (100 francs for those under 15).

If you're arriving from an EU country, you may be required to declare all goods and prove that anything over the standard limit is for personal consumption. Since January 1993, however, limits and customs tariffs on goods carried within the EU have been eliminated.

Any amount of French or foreign currency may be brought into France, but foreign currencies converted into francs may be reconverted into a foreign currency only up to the equivalent of 5,000 francs.

ENTERING THE U.S.

You may bring home $400 worth of foreign goods duty-free if you've been out of the country for at least 48 hours and haven't already used the $400 allowance or any part of it in the past 30 days.

Travelers 21 and older may bring back 1 liter of alcohol duty-free. In addition, regardless of your age, you are allowed 200 cigarettes and 100 non-Cuban cigars. (At press time, a federal rule restricting tobacco access to persons 18 years and older did not apply to importation.) Antiques, which the U.S. Customs Service defines as objects more than 100 years old, enter duty-free, as do original works of art done entirely by hand, including paintings, drawings, and sculptures.

You may also send packages home duty-free: up to $200 worth of goods for personal use, with a limit of one parcel per addressee per day (and no alcohol or tobacco products or perfume worth more than $5); label the package PERSONAL USE, and attach a list of its contents and their retail value. Do not label the package UNSOLICITED GIFT, or your duty-free exemption will drop to $100. Mailed items do not affect your duty-free allowance on your return.

INFORMATION➤ **U.S. Customs Service** (✉ Box 7407, Washington, DC 20044, ☎ 202/927–6724 for inquiries; ✉ Commissioner's Office, 1301 Constitution Ave. NW, Washington, DC 20229 for complaints; ✉ Resource Management, 1301 Constitution Ave. NW, Washington DC, 20229, ☎ 202/927–0540 for equipment registration).

ENTERING CANADA

If you've been out of Canada for at least 7 days you may bring in C$500 worth of goods duty-free. If you've been away for fewer than 7 days but more than 48 hours, the duty-free allowance drops to C$200; if your trip lasts 24–48 hours, the allowance is C$50. You may not pool allowances with family members. Goods claimed under the C$500 exemption may follow you by mail; those claimed under the lesser exemptions must accompany you.

Alcohol and tobacco products may be included in the 7-day and 48-hour exemptions but not in the 24-hour exemption. If you meet the age requirements of the province or territory through which you reenter Canada you may bring in, duty-free, 1.14 liters (40 imperial ounces) of wine or liquor *or* 24 12-ounce cans or bottles of beer or ale. If you are 16 or older you may bring in, duty-free, 200 cigarettes and 50 cigars; these items must accompany you.

You may send an unlimited number of gifts worth up to C$60 each duty-free to Canada. Label the package UNSOLICITED GIFT—VALUE UNDER $60. Alcohol and tobacco are excluded.

INFORMATION➤ **Revenue Canada** (✉ 2265 St. Laurent Blvd. S, Ottawa, Ontario K1G 4K3, ☎ 613/993–0534, 800/461–9999 in Canada).

ENTERING THE U.K.

If your journey was wholly within EU countries you needn't pass through customs when you return to the United Kingdom. If you plan to bring back large quantities of alcohol or tobacco, check on EU limits beforehand.

INFORMATION➤ **HM Customs and Excise** (✉ Dorset House, Stamford St., London SE1 9NG, ☎ 0171/202–4227).

DISABILITIES & ACCESSIBILITY

ACCESS IN PARIS

Though it has a long way to go, Paris ranks above many European cities in its ability to accommodate travelers with mobility problems. Most sidewalks now have low curbs, and most arrondissements have public rest rooms and telephone boxes that are wheelchair-accessible. Taxi drivers are required by law to assist travelers with disabilities in and out of vehicles. In addition, most métro stations are wheelchair-accessible.

LOCAL RESOURCES➤ An RER and métro access guide is available at most stations, as well as from **Paris Transit Authority (RATP) kiosks** (✉ 53 bis quai des Grands Augustins, 6ᵉ; ✉ pl. de la Madeleine, 8ᵉ, ☎ 08–36–68–41–14).

DISCOUNTS & DEALS

AIRLINE TICKETS➤ ☎ 800/FLY-4-LESS.

HOTEL ROOMS➤ **Hotels Plus** (☎ 800/235–0909). **Hotel Reservations Network (HRN)** (☎ 800/964–6835). **International Marketing & Travel Concepts (IMTC)** (☎ 800/790–4682).

SENIOR-CITIZEN DISCOUNTS

To qualify for age-related discounts, **mention your senior-citizen status up front** when booking hotel reservations (not when checking out) and before you're seated in restaurants (not when paying the bill). Note that discounts may be limited to certain menus, days, or hours. When renting a car, **ask about promotional car-rental discounts,** which can be cheaper than senior-citizen rates.

STUDENT DISCOUNTS

Students are a noticeable presence in the capital, where intellectuals are the French equivalent of American movie stars. The area surrounding the Sorbonne in the bohemian Latin Quarter is filled with students discoursing in smoke-filled cafés or browsing in crowded bookshops. For a detailed listing of deals for students in Paris, ask for the brochure *"Jeunes à Paris"* from the main tourist office (⊠ 127 av. des Champs-Elysées, ☎ 01–49–52–53–54). Also try **Usit Voyages** (⊠ 12 rue Vivienne, 2ᵉ, ☎ 01–42–44–14–00) for information on hostels, cheap accommodations, and student travel. *France-USA Contacts,* a twice-monthly publication with useful information for students, is available free in restaurants and in most American and British bookstores.

STUDENT IDs AND SERVICES➤ **Council on International Educational Exchange** (⊠ CIEE, 205 E. 42nd St., 14th floor, New York, NY 10017, ☎ 212/822–2600 or 888/268–6245, FAX 212/822–2699), for mail orders only, in the United States. **Travel Cuts** (⊠ 187 College St., Toronto, Ontario M5T 1P7, ☎ 416/979–2406 or 800/667–2887) in Canada.

ELECTRICITY

To use your U.S.-purchased electric-powered equipment, **bring a converter and adapter.** The electrical current in France is 220 volts, 50 cycles alternating current (AC); wall outlets take Continental-type plugs, with two round prongs.

If your appliances are dual-voltage, you'll need only an adapter. Don't use 110-volt outlets, marked FOR SHAVERS ONLY, for high-wattage appliances such as blow-dryers. Most laptops operate equally well on 110 and 220 volts and so require only an adapter.

EMBASSIES & EMERGENCIES

EMBASSIES➤ **U.S. Embassy** (⊠ 2 av. Gabriel, 8ᵉ, ☎ 01–43–12–22–22). **Canadian Embassy** (⊠ 35 av. Montaigne, 8ᵉ, ☎ 01–44–43–29–00). **British Embassy** (⊠ 35 rue du Faubourg St-Honoré, 8ᵉ, ☎ 01–44–51–31–00).

EMERGENCIES➤ Fire (☎ 18); locals tend to call the fire department for any type of emergency as it has fully trained medical teams and is very efficient. **Police** (☎ 17). **Ambulance** (☎ 15 or ☎ 01–45–67–50–50). **Doctor** (☎ 01–47–07–77–77). **Dentist** (☎ 01–43–37–51–00).

HOSPITALS➤ **The American Hospital** (✉ 63 bd. Victor Hugo, Neuilly, ☎ 01–46–41–25–25) has a 24-hour emergency service. **The Hertford British Hospital** (✉ 3 rue Barbès, Levallois-Perret, ☎ 01–46–39–22–22) also offers a 24-hour service.

24-HOUR PHARMACIES➤ **Dhéry** (✉ Galerie des Champs, 84 av. des Champs-Elysées, 8ᵉ, ☎ 01–45–62–02–41) is open 24 hours. **Pharmacie Matignon** (✉ rue Jean Mermoz, at the Rond-Point de Champs-Elysées, 8ᵉ) is open daily until 2 AM. **Pharmacie des Arts** (✉ 106 bd. Montparnasse, 14ᵉ) is open daily until midnight.

HEALTH

MEDICAL PLANS

No one plans to get sick while traveling, but it happens, so **consider signing up with a medical-assistance company.** Members get doctor referrals, emergency evacuation or repatriation, 24-hour telephone hot lines for medical consultation, cash for emergencies, and other personal and legal assistance. Coverage varies by plan, so **review the benefits carefully.**

MEDICAL-ASSISTANCE COMPANIES➤ **International SOS Assistance** (✉ Box 11568, Philadelphia, PA 19116, ☎ 215/244–1500 or 800/523–8930; ✉ Box 466, pl. Bonaventure, Montréal, Québec H5A 1C1, ☎ 514/874–7674 or 800/363–0263; ✉ 7 Old Lodge Pl., St. Margarets, Twickenham TW1 1RQ, England, ☎ 0181/744–0033). **MEDEX Assistance Corporation** (✉ Box 5375, Timonium, MD 21094, ☎ 410/453–6300 or 800/537–2029).

Traveler's Emergency Network (✉ 3100 Tower Blvd., Suite 1000B, Durham, NC 27707, ☎ 919/490–6055 or 800/275–4836, ℻ 919/493–8262). **TravMed** (✉ Box 5375, Timonium, MD 21094, ☎ 410/453–6380 or 800/732–5309). **Worldwide Assistance Services** (✉ 1133 15th St. NW, Suite 400, Washington, DC 20005, ☎ 202/331–1609 or 800/821–2828, ℻ 202/828–5896).

MONEY

The units of currency in France are the franc (fr) and the centime. Bills are in denominations of 500, 200, 100, 50, and 20 francs. Coins are 20, 10, 5, 2, and 1 francs and 50, 20, 10, and 5 centimes. Note that the old 10-franc coin has been replaced by a smaller, two-tone version. At press time, the exchange rate was about 5 francs to the U.S. dollar, 3.75 to the Canadian dollar, and 7.75 to the pound sterling.

ATMS

Before leaving home, **make sure that your credit cards have been programmed for ATM use in Paris.** Note that Discover is accepted mostly in the United States. Local bank cards often do not work overseas or may access only your checking account; **ask your bank about a MasterCard/Cirrus or Visa debit card,** which works like a bank card but can be used at any ATM displaying a MasterCard/Cirrus or Visa logo. These cards, too, may tap only your checking account; check with your bank about their policy.

ATM LOCATIONS➤ **Cirrus** (☎ 800/424–7787). A list of **Plus** locations is available at your local bank.

CURRENCY EXCHANGE

For the most favorable rates, **change money at banks.** Although fees charged for ATM transactions may be higher abroad than at home, Cirrus and Plus exchange rates are excellent, because they are based on wholesale rates offered only by major banks. You won't do as well at exchange booths in airports or rail and bus stations, in hotels, in restaurants, or in stores, although you may find their hours more convenient. To avoid lines at airport exchange booths, **get a small amount of local currency before you leave home.**

EXCHANGE SERVICES➤ **International Currency Express** (☎ 888/842–0880 on the East Coast or 888/278–6628 on the West Coast for telephone orders). **Thomas Cook Currency Services** (☎ 800/287–7362 for telephone orders and retail locations).

TRAVELER'S CHECKS

Whether or not to buy traveler's checks depends on where you are headed. **Take cash if your trip includes rural areas** and small towns, traveler's checks to cities. If your checks are lost or stolen, they can usually be replaced within 24 hours. To ensure a speedy refund, buy your checks yourself (don't ask someone else to make the purchase). When making a claim for stolen or lost checks, the person who bought the checks should make the call.

PASSPORTS & VISAS

Once your travel plans are confirmed, **check the expiration date of your passport.** It's also a good idea to **make photocopies of the data page;** leave one copy with someone at home and keep another with you, separate from your passport. If you lose your passport, promptly call the nearest embassy or consulate and the local police; having a copy of the data page can speed replacement.

U.S. CITIZENS

All U.S. citizens, even infants, need only a valid passport to enter France for stays of up to 90 days.

INFORMATION➤ **Office of Passport Services** (☎ 202/647–0518).

CANADIANS

You need only a valid passport to enter France for stays of up to 90 days.

INFORMATION➤ **Passport Office** (☎ 819/994–3500 or 800/567–6868).

U.K. CITIZENS

Citizens of the United Kingdom need only a valid passport to enter France for stays of up to 90 days.

INFORMATION➤ **London Passport Office** (☎ 0990/21010) for fees and documentation requirements and to request an emergency passport.

PUBLIC TRANSPORTATION

Paris is relatively small as capital cities go, and many of its **prize monuments and museums are within easy walking distance of one another.** Walking is also a wonderful way of discovering the many pedestrian streets, beautiful courtyards, and other hidden pleasures off the beaten path. The most convenient form of public transportation is the métro, with stops every few hundred yards. Buses are a slower but more pleasant alternative, as you see more of the city. Taxis are relatively inexpensive and convenient, but not always easy to find. Even in heavily touristed areas, you can't count on snagging one, especially on a Saturday night after the last métro. Private car travel within Paris is best avoided; parking is extremely difficult.

BY BUS

Travel by bus is a convenient, scenic way to get around the city, although it's slower than the métro. Paris buses are green and white; route number and destination are marked in front and major stopping-places along the sides. Most routes operate from 7 AM to 8:30 PM; some continue to midnight. Ten Noctambus, or night buses, operate hourly (1:30–5:30 AM) between Châtelet and various nearby suburbs; you can stop them by hailing them at any point on their route. The brown bus shelters, topped by red and yellow circular signs, contain timetables and route maps. Paris-Visite/Formule 1 passes are valid, otherwise it costs 30 francs. Regular buses accept métro tickets, or you can buy a single ticket on board. You need to show (but not punch) weekly, monthly, and Paris-Visite/Formule 1 (☞ By Métro, *below*) tickets to the driver as you get on. If you have individual tickets, you should be prepared to punch one or more tickets in the red and gray machines on board the bus.

Check out the Montmartrobus for a tour of some of the most charming streets around the *butte* (mound). The terminus is at the Pigalle metro station. The Balabus, another public bus that follows an interesting route, runs between May and September and is a good way to see the major sights. (Terminus: La Défense or Gare de Lyon.)

BY MÉTRO

Métro stations are recognizable either by a large yellow *M* within a circle or by the distinctive curly green Art Nouveau railings and archway bearing the full title (Métropolitain). **The métro is the most efficient way to get around Paris** and is so clearly marked at all points that it's easy to find your way without asking for directions.

Thirteen métro lines crisscross Paris and the suburbs, and you are seldom more than 500 yards from the nearest station. It is essential to know the name of the last station on the line you take, as this name appears on all signs. A connection (you can make as many as you like on one ticket) is called a *correspondance*. At junction stations, illuminated orange signs bearing the name of the line terminus appear over the correct corridors for each *correspondance*. Illuminated blue signs marked *sortie* indicate the station exit. Don't pass through any of the gates or *limites,* as your tickets are only valid inside these.

The métro service starts at 5:30 AM and continues until 1 AM, when the last train on each line reaches its terminus. Some lines and stations in the less salubrious parts of Paris are risky at night, in particular Lines 2 and 13. But in general, the métro is relatively safe throughout, providing you don't walk around with your wallet hanging out of your back pocket or (especially women) travel alone late at night. The biggest nuisances you're likely to encounter will be the wine-swigging *clochards* (tramps) blurting out drunken songs as they bed down on platform benches.

The métro network connects at several points in Paris with the RER (Réseau Express Régional, or the Regional Express Network). RER trains, which race across Paris from suburb to suburb, are a sort of supersonic métro and can be great time-savers.

All métro tickets and passes are valid for RER *and* bus travel within Paris. Métro tickets cost 8 francs each; a *carnet* (10 tickets for 46 francs) is a better value. If you're staying for a week or more and plan to use the métro frequently, the best deal is the weekly (*coupon jaune*) or monthly (*carte orange*) ticket, sold according to zone. Zones 1 and 2 cover the entire métro network; tickets cost 72 francs a week or 243 francs a month. If you plan to take suburban trains to visit places in the Ile-de-France, consider a four-zone (Versailles, St-Germain-en-Laye; 126 francs a week) or six-zone (Rambouillet, Fontainebleau; 170 francs a week) ticket. For these weekly/monthly tickets, you will need a pass (available from rail and major métro stations) and a passport-size photograph.

Alternatively, there are one-day (Formule 1) and three- and five-day (Paris Visite) unlimited travel tickets for the métro, bus, and RER. Their advantage is that, unlike the *coupon jaune,* which is good from Monday morning to Sunday evening, Formule 1 and Paris Visite passes are valid starting any day of the week and also give you discounts on a limited number of museums and tourist attractions. The price is 40 (one-day), 70 (two-day), 105 (three-day), and 165 (five-day) francs for Paris only; 170, 230, and 315 francs, respectively, for suburbs including Versailles, St-Germain-en-Laye, and Disneyland Paris.

Access to métro and RER platforms is through an automatic ticket barrier. Slide your ticket in and pick it up as it pops out. Be certain to keep your ticket during your journey; you'll need it to leave the RER system and in case you run into any green-clad ticket inspectors, who will fine you if you don't present your ticket.

Maps of the métro/RER network are available free from any métro station and in many hotels. They are also posted on every platform, as are maps of the bus network. To help you find your way around Paris, we suggest you **buy a Plan de Paris par Arrondissement** (about 40 francs), a city guide with separate maps of each dis-

trict, including the whereabouts of métro stations and an index of street names. They're on sale in newsstands, bookstores, stationers, and drugstores. To determine the arrondissement of an address, here's a **hint: The last two digits of Paris zip codes are the number of the arrondissement**; for example, the zip code 75005 indicates an address in the 5th arrondissement, 75011 is in the 11th arrondissement, and so forth. In addresses in this guide, arrondissements are noted as follows: "1er" indicates the 1st arrondissement; "2^e," the second; "3^e," the third; and so on.

TAXES

HOTEL

Restaurant and hotel prices must by law include taxes and service charges: If these appear as additional items on your bill, you should complain.

SALES

All taxes must be included in affixed prices in France.

VAT

VAT (value added tax, known in France as TVA), at a standard rate of 20.6% (33% for luxury goods), is included in the price of many goods, but foreigners are often entitled to a refund (☞ Chapter 6).

TELEPHONES

The country code for France is 33. When dialing a French number from abroad, drop the initial 0 from the local area code.

CALLING HOME

To call out of France, dial 00 and wait for the tone, then dial the country code (1 for the United States and Canada, 44 for the United Kingdom) and the area code (minus any initial 0) and number. Expect to be overcharged if you make calls from your hotel. With the liberalization of the French telecommunications market, phone charges have dropped significantly. Approximate daytime rates, per minute, are 5 francs to the United States and Canada (8 AM–9:30 PM), and 4 francs to the United Kingdom (2 PM–8 PM); reduced rates at other time intervals, per minute, are 4 francs to the United States and Canada and 3 francs to the United Kingdom.

Before you go, **find out the local access codes** for your destinations. AT&T, MCI, and Sprint long-distance services make calling home relatively convenient, but you may find the local access number blocked in many hotel rooms. First ask the hotel operator to connect you. If the hotel operator balks, ask for an international operator, or dial the international operator yourself. One way to improve your odds of getting connected to your long-distance carrier is to travel with more than one company's calling card (a hotel may block Sprint, for example, but not MCI). If all else fails, call your phone company collect

in the United States or call from a pay phone in the hotel lobby.

To Obtain Access Codes➤ **AT&T USADirect** (☎ 800/874–4000). **MCI Call USA** (☎ 800/444–4444). **Sprint Express** (☎ 800/793–1153).

OPERATORS AND INFORMATION

To find a number within France or to request information, dial 12. For international inquiries, dial 00–33 plus the country code.

PAY PHONES

The French telephone system is modern and efficient. A local call costs 1 franc for every 3 minutes. Call-boxes are plentiful; they're found at post offices, in métro stations, and often in cafés.

Most French pay phones are now operated by cards (*télécartes*), which you can buy from post offices, *tabacs* (tabacco shops/newsstands), and métro stations (the cost is 40 francs for 50 units; 96 francs for 120 units). These cards will save you time and money. In cafés you can still find pay phones that operate with 1-, 2-, and 5-franc coins (1 franc for local calls). Lift the receiver, place your coin(s) in the appropriate slots, and dial. Unused coins are returned when you hang up.

In October 1996, phone numbers in France changed because of a need for more telephone lines. France-Télécom added to all phone numbers a prefix of two digits, determined by zone: Paris and the Ile-de-France, 01 (replacing the 16 + 1); the northwest, 02; the northeast, 03; the southeast, 04; and the southwest, 05.

TRAIN TRAVEL

See Métro, *above*.

For schedules and other information contact the **SNCF** (✉ 88 rue St-Lazare, 75009 Paris, ☎ 08–36–35–35–35).

FROM THE U.K.

British Rail (☎ 0171/834–2345) has four daily departures from London's Victoria Station, all linking with the Dover–Calais/Boulogne ferry services through to Paris. There is also an overnight service on the Newhaven–Dieppe ferry. Journey time is about eight hours. Credit-card bookings are accepted by phone or in person at a British Rail Travel Centre (☞ *Also* The Channel Tunnel, *above*).

TRAVEL AGENCIES

A good travel agent puts your needs first. **Look for an agency that specializes in your destination, has been in business at least five years, and emphasizes customer service.** If you want an agency-organized package or tour, choose an agency that's a member of the National Tour Association or the United States Tour Operator's Association.

LOCAL AGENT REFERRALS➤ **American Society of Travel Agents** (ASTA; ✉ 1101 King St., Suite 200, Alexandria, VA 22314, ☎ 703/739–2782, FAX 703/684–8319). **Alliance of Canadian Travel Associations** (✉ Suite 201, 1729 Bank St., Ottawa, Ontario K1V 7Z5, ☎ 613/521–0474, FAX 613/521–0805). **Association of British Travel Agents** (✉ 55–57 Newman St., London W1P 4AH, ☎ 0171/637–2444, FAX 0171/637–0713).

VISITOR INFORMATION

FRENCH GOVERNMENT TOURIST OFFICE➤ **U.S. Nationwide** (☎ 900/990–0040; costs 50¢ per minute). **New York City** (✉ 444 Madison Ave., 10022, ☎ 212/838–7800). **Chicago** (✉ 676 N. Michigan Ave., 60611, ☎ 312/751–7800). **Beverly Hills** (✉ 9454 Wilshire Blvd., 90212, ☎ 310/271–6665, FAX 310/276–2835). **Canada** (✉ 1981 Ave. McGill College, Suite 490, Montréal, Québec H3A 2W9, ☎ 514/288–4264, FAX 514/845–4868; ✉ 30 St. Patrick St., Suite 700, Toronto, Ontario M5T 3A3, ☎ 416/491–7622, FAX 416/979–7587). **U.K.** (✉ 178 Piccadilly, London W1V OAL, ☎ 0891/244–123; 50p per minute charge).

WHEN TO GO

The major tourist season in France stretches from Easter to mid-September, but Paris has much to offer in every season. In the early spring, the city can be disappointingly damp; June is delightful, with good weather and plenty of cultural and other attractions. July and August can be sultry. Moreover, many theaters and some of the smaller restaurants and shops close for at least four weeks in August. September is ideal. Cultural life revives after the summer break, and sunny weather often continues through the first half of October. The ballet and theater are in full swing in November, but the weather is part wet-and-cold, part bright-and-sunny.

December is dominated by the *fêtes de fin d'année* (end-of-year festivities), with splendid displays in food shops and restaurants and a busy theater, ballet, and opera season into January. February and March are the worst months, weatherwise, but with the coming of Easter, Paris starts to look beautiful again.

What follow are the average daily maximum and minimum temperatures for Paris.

Climate in Paris

Jan.	43F	6C	May	68F	20C	Sept.	70F	21C
	34	1		49	10		53	12
Feb.	45F	7C	June	73F	23C	Oct.	60F	16C
	34	1		55	13		46	8
Mar.	54F	12C	July	76F	25C	Nov.	50F	10C
	39	4		58	14		40	5
Apr.	60F	16C	Aug.	75F	24C	Dec.	44F	7C
	43	6		58	14		36	2

1 Destination: Paris

PARIS À LA PARISIENNE

T IS MIDNIGHT at the neighborhood brasserie. Waiters swathed in starchy white glance discreetly at their watches as a family—mother, son, and wife—sip the last of a bottle of Chiroubles and scrape up the remains of their steak tartare on silverware dexterously poised with arched wrists. They are all wearing scarves: The mother's is a classic silk *carré*, tastefully folded at the throat; the wife's is Indian gauze and glitters; the son's is wool and hangs like a prayer shawl over his black turtleneck. Finished, they stir their coffee without looking. They smoke: the mother, Gitanes; the son, Marlboros; the wife rolls her own from a silver case. Alone, they act out their personal theater, uncontrived and unobserved, their Doisneauesque tableau reflected only in the etched-glass mirrors around them, enhanced by the sobriety of their dress and the pallor of their Gallic skin.

Whoever first said that "God found Paris too perfect, so he invented the Parisians," had it wrong. This extraordinary maquette of a city, with its landscape of mansards and chimneys, its low-slung bridges and vast boulevards, is nothing but a rough-sketched stage set that drinks its color from the lifeblood of those infamous Parisians whom everyone claims to hate, but whom everyone loves to emulate.

Mythologized for their arrogance, charm, and savoir faire—as well as their disdain for the foreigners they find genetically incapable of sharing these characteristics—the Parisians continue to mesmerize. For the generations of American and English voyeurs who have ventured curiously, enviously into countless mirrored brasseries, downed numerous bottles of *cuvée maison,* fumbled at nautical knots in newly bought scarves, even suffered squashed berets and unfiltered Gauloises, the Parisian remains inimitable—and infinitely fascinating.

Alternately patronizing and self-effacing, they move through their big-city lives with enviable style and urban grit. They are chronically thin, despite the truckloads of beef stew, pâté, and *tarte tatine* they consume without blushing. They still make the cigarette look glamorous—and a graceful bit of stage business indispensable to good talk—in spite of the gasmask levels of smoke they generate. They stride over bridges aloof to the monuments framed in every sweeping perspective, yet they discourse—lightly, charmingly—on Racine, NATO, and the latest ruling of the Académie Française. They are proud, practical, often witty and always chic, from the thrift-shop style of the Sorbonne student to the Chanel suit on the thin shoulders of a well-boned *dame d'un certain age.*

Ferociously (with some justice) in love with their own culture—theater, literature, film, art, architecture, haute cuisine, and haute couture—Parisians worship France as ardently as New Yorkers dismiss America. While Manhattanites berate the nonentities west of the Hudson, Parisians romanticize the rest of France, making an art of the weekend foray and the regional vacation: Why should we go *à l'étranger* (abroad) when we have the Dordogne, the Auvergne, and Bretagne?

And for all their vulnerability to what they frame as the "American Assault," for every Disney store, action film, and McDonald's in Paris (not to mention Benetton and Laura Ashley, and France's own Celio, Orcade, and Descamps chains), there is a plethora of unique shops selling all-white blouses, African bracelets, dog jackets, and Art Deco jewelry.

And for every commercial bookstore chain there are five tiny *librairies* selling tooled-leather encyclopedias, collections of out-of-print plays, and yellow paperbacks lovingly pressed in waxed paper. The famous *bouquinistes* hover like squatters along the Seine, their folding metal boxes opening to showcase a treasure trove of old magazines, scholarly journals, and hand-colored botanical prints that flap from clothespins in the wind. Yet they are not nomads, these bouquinistes: Dormant through winter, their metal stands are fixtures as permanent and respectable as those of the medieval merchants that built shops along the Pont Neuf.

BUT IN SPITE of their fierce individuality, Parisians also demand that certain conformities be followed. And here the gap between native and visitor widens. If Parisians treat tourists a bit like occupying forces—disdainfully selling them Beaujolais-Nouveau in July, seating them by the kitchen doors, refusing to understand honest attempts at French—they have formed their opinions based on bitter experience. The meal is a sacred ritual here and diverging from the norm is tantamount to disgrace.

Doing as the Parisians do, you can go a long way toward closing the gap of disdain. When dining, for example, give yourself over to the meal. Order a kir as an aperitif, instead of a whiskey or beer. Drink wine or mineral water with your meal; more international incidents have occurred over requests for tap water or Coke than over the Suez Canal.

THE WINE WILL come chilled, aired, and ready for tasting with the respect usually reserved for a holy relic. Enjoy each course, sipping, discussing, digesting leisurely; the waiter will not be pressed by hurried tourists. When you're done eating, align your silverware on the plate (a sign for the waiter to clear). Cheese can be the climax of the meal, well worth skipping dessert if necessary, and a magnificent way to finish the wine. Have your coffee after dessert and, without exception, black with sugar; a milky froth will not do on a full stomach.

Ask for *l'addition;* the waiter will not commit the gaffe of bringing the check uninvited. And no matter how deeply you enter into your role as Parisian manqué avoid saying "Garçon!" These are rules that apply at the most unassuming corner bistro and the grandest three-star restaurant; following them can thaw the waiterly chill that can render a meal unforgettable—for all the wrong reasons—and can make for meals that are memorable as an evening at the Opéra Bastille, complete with sets and choreography.

By matching that Parisian passion for the complete, the correct, the comme il faut, your own experience will be all the more authentic. Having eaten with proper reverence, keep your sightseeing agenda at the same lofty level. If you go to the Louvre, spend the day; do not lope through the wide corridors in search of *La Joconde* (Mona Lisa). You can leave for a three-hour lunch, if you choose, and come back with the same ticket, even avoiding the lines by reentering via the Passage de Richelieu. If time won't allow an all-day survey, do as the locals do: Choose an era and immerse yourself. Then take a break and plunge into another. Eavesdrop on a guided tour. Go back and look at a painting again. And take the time to stare at the ceilings: The architecture alone of this historic monument merits a day's tour.

As you apply yourself to the Parisian experience in spirit, diverge in fact: Walk. The natives may prefer to sit in a café or even hurry straight home by métro (*"métro, boulot, do-do"*—"métro, work, sleep"—as the saying goes). You, as a visitor, are obliged to wander down tortuous medieval streets; up vast boulevards; over bridges that open up broad perspectives on illuminated monuments that outnumber even those in Rome.

They are all there, the clichés of Paris romance: The moon over the Seine reflected in the wake of the bateaux mouches; the steps Leslie Caron blushed down in *An American in Paris;* the lovers kissing under the lime tree pollards. But there are surprises, too: a troop of hunting horns striking unearthly sonorities under a resonant bridge; flocks of wild geese flying low over the towers of Notre-Dame; and a ragged expatriate-writer leaving a well-scraped plat du jour on the table as he bolts away from the bill. (*C'est dommage:* He would have been well-fed by Ragueneau, the baker-writer in *Cyrano de Bergerac* who opened his Paris pastry shop to starving poets.)

The more resourceful you are, the more surprises you will unearth in your Paris wanderings. Follow the strains of Lully into a chamber orchestra rehearsal in St-Julien-le-Pauvre; if you're quiet and still, you may not be asked to leave. Brave the smoking lounge at intermission at the Comédie-Française and you'll find the battered leather chair that the young actor Molière sat in as *L'Invalide Imaginaire.* Take the métro to *L'Armée du Salut* (Salvation Army) in the 13ᵉ arrondissement, and you'll not only find Art Deco percolators and hand-knit stockings, but you'll also be inside the futuristic curves of a 1933 Le Corbusier masterwork.

Tear yourself away from the big-name museums and you'll discover a world of small galleries. Go in: You don't have to press your nose to the glass. The exhibits are constantly changing and you can always find one relevant to Paris—Frank Horvat's photos of Pigalle or a Christo retrospective, including the Pont Neuf wrappings. It is worth buying one of the weekly guides—*Pariscope, Les Officiels des Spectacles, Figaroscope*—and browsing through it over your *café crème* and croissant.

RESOURCEFULNESS, after all, is a sign of enthusiasm and appreciation—for when you are well-informed and acutely tuned in to the nuances of the city, you can approach it as a connoisseur. Then you can peacefully coexist with Parisians, partaking, in their passion for this marvelous old city, from the same plate of cultural riches. Hemingway, as usual, put it succinctly: "It was always pleasant crossing bridges in Paris." Cultural bridges, too.

Bon Séjour à Paris.

— Nancy Coons

A frequent contributor to Fodor's, Nancy Coons has written on food and culture for *National Geographic Traveler, Wall Street Journal, Opera News,* and *European Travel & Life.* Based in Luxembourg and France since 1987, she now works out of her 300-year-old farmhouse in Lorraine, which she shares with her husband and two daughters.

2 Exploring Paris

Updated
by Simon
Hewitt

A CITY OF VAST, NOBLE PERSPECTIVES and winding, hidden streets, Paris remains a combination of the pompous and the intimate. Whether you've come looking for sheer physical beauty, cultural and artistic diversions, history, or simply local color, you will find it here in abundance.

The French capital is also a practical city: It is relatively small as capitals go, with many of its major sites and museums within walking distance of one another. The city's principal tourist axis is less than 6½ km (4 mi) long, running parallel to the north bank of the Seine from the Arc de Triomphe to the Bastille. In fact, the best method of getting to know Paris is on foot, although public transportation—particularly the métro subway system—is excellent. Buy a *Plan de Paris* booklet: a city map-guide with a street-name index that also shows métro stations. Note that all métro stations have a detailed neighborhood map just inside the entrance.

Paris owes both its development and much of its visual appeal to the river Seine, which weaves through its heart. Each bank of the Seine has its own personality; the *Rive Droite* (Right Bank), with its spacious boulevards and formal buildings, generally has a more sober and genteel feeling than the more carefree and bohemian *Rive Gauche* (Left Bank) to the south. The historical and geographical heart of the city is Notre-Dame Cathedral on the Ile de la Cité, the larger of the Seine's two islands (the other is the Ile St-Louis).

Our coverage of Paris is divided into eight neighborhoods. There are several "musts" that you may not want to miss: the Eiffel Tower, the Champs-Elysées, the Louvre, and Notre-Dame. A few monuments and museums close for lunch, between noon and 2, and many are closed on either Monday or Tuesday. Check before you set off. Admission prices listed are for adults, but often there are special rates for students, children, and senior citizens.

FROM THE EIFFEL TOWER TO THE LOUVRE

Between the Eiffel Tower and the Louvre lies the grand, opulent Paris of wide avenues and plush hotels. This is an area of dazzling vistas, stellar museums, superb window-shopping, and unbeatable monument-gazing. Fashion shops, jewelers, art galleries, and deluxe hotels proliferate. Local charm is not a feature of this exclusive sector of western Paris; it's beautiful and rich—and a little impersonal. The French moan that it's losing its character, and, as you notice the number of fast-food joints along the Champs-Elysées, you'll know what they mean—though renovation has gone some way to restoring the street's legendary elegance.

The Arc de Triomphe stands foursquare at the top of the most famous street in the city: the Champs-Elysées, site of most French national celebrations. It's the last leg of the Tour de France bicycle race on the third or fourth Sunday in July and the site of vast ceremonies on Bastille Day (July 14) and Armistice Day (November 11). Its trees are often decked with the French *tricolore* and foreign flags to mark visits from heads of state.

Numbers in the margin correspond to numbers on the Eiffel Tower to Trocadéro and Arc de Triomphe to Louvre maps; these numbers indicate a suggested path for sightseeing.

Sights to See

★ ⑧ **Arc de Triomphe.** This colossal, 164-foot Triumphal Arch was planned by Napoléon—who believed himself to be the direct heir to the Roman emperors—to celebrate his military successes. But empires come and go, and Napoléon's had been gone for more than 20 years before the Arc de Triomphe was finally finished, in 1836. It has some magnificent sculpture by François Rude, such as the *Departure of the Volunteers,* better known as *La Marseillaise,* situated to the right of the arch when viewed from the Champs-Elysées. There is a small museum halfway up the arch devoted to its history. France's Unknown Soldier is buried beneath the archway; the flame is rekindled every evening

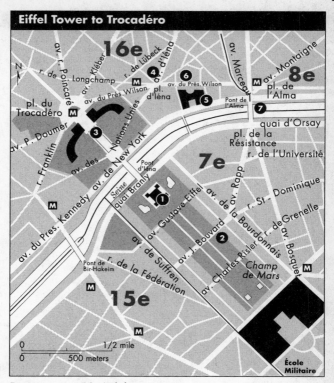

Eiffel Tower to Trocadéro

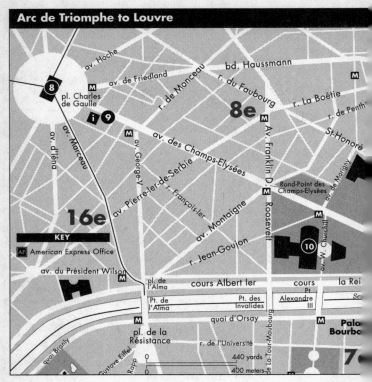

Arc de Triomphe to Louvre

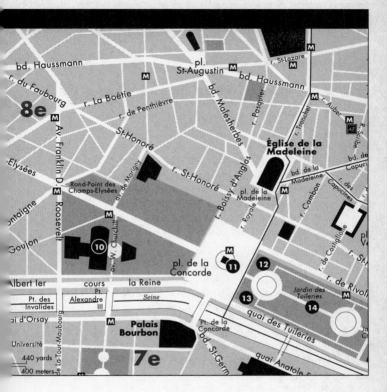

bd. Haussmann

r. du Faubourg

8e

r. La Boétie

r. de Penthièvre

Av. Franklin D. Roosevelt

St-Honoré

pl.
St-Augustin

bd. Haussmann

r. St-Lazare

bd. Malesherbes

r. Pasquier

r. Tronchet

r. Auber

r. Scribe

**Église de la
Madeleine**

bd. de la
Madeleine

bd. de
Capuci

r. des
Capucines

Elysées

ontaine

Rond-Point des
Champs-Elysées

r. St-Honoré

r. Boissy d'Anglas

pl. de la
Madeleine

r. Royale

r. Cambon

r. de Castiglione

r. St

Goujon

av. de Marigny

av. W. Churchill

10

**pl. de la
Concorde**

11

12

13

14

Jardin des
Tuileries

r. de Rivoli

Albert 1er

cours

la Reine

Pt. des
Invalides

Pt.
Alexandre
III

Seine

ai d'Orsay

**Palais
Bourbon**

Pt. de la
Concorde

quai des Tuileries

r. de la Tour-Maubourg

Université

7e

bd. St-Germ

quai Anatole F

440 yards

400 meters

at 6:30. ⊠ *pl. Charles-de-Gaulle,* ☎ *01–43–80–31–31.*
🎟 *32 frs.* ☉ *Daily 10–5:30; winter, daily 10–5; closed public holidays. Métro or RER: Etoile.*

🖐 ❼ **Bateaux Mouches.** These popular motorboats set off on their hour-long tours of Paris waters regularly (every half hour in summer) from place de l'Alma, heading east to the Ile St-Louis and then back west, past the Eiffel Tower, as far as the Allée des Cygnes and its miniature version of the Statue of Liberty. ⊠ *pl. de l'Alma,* ☎ *01–40–76–99–99.* 🎟 *40 frs. Métro: Alma-Marceau.*

🖐 ❷ **Champ de Mars.** This long, formal garden, landscaped at the start of the century, lies between the Eiffel Tower and École Militaire. It was previously used as a parade ground and was the site of the World Exhibitions of 1867, 1889 (date of the construction of the Eiffel Tower), and 1900. *Métro: École Militaire; RER: Champ-de-Mars.*

Champs-Elysées. The 2-km (1¼-mi) Champs-Elysées was originally laid out in the 1660s by the landscape gardener Le Nôtre as a garden sweeping away from the Tuileries. You won't see many signs of those pastoral origins as you stroll past the cafés, airline offices, car showrooms, movie theaters, and chic arcades that occupy its upper half. In an attempt to reestablish this thoroughfare as one of the world's most beautiful avenues, the city planted extra trees, refurbished Art Nouveau newsstands, built underground parking to alleviate congestion, and clamped down on garish storefronts. *Métro: George-V, Franklin-D.-Roosevelt.*

★ 🖐 ❶ **Eiffel Tower.** Known to the French as La Tour Eiffel (pronounced F.L.), Paris's most famous landmark was built by Gustave Eiffel for the World Exhibition of 1889, the centennial of the French Revolution, and was still in good shape to celebrate its own 100th birthday. Such was Eiffel's engineering wizardry that even in the strongest winds his tower never sways more than 4½ inches. Its colossal bulk exudes a feeling of mighty permanence—so you may have trouble believing that it nearly became 7,000 tons of scrap iron when its concession expired in 1909. Only its potential use as a radio antenna saved the day; it now bristles with a forest of radio and television transmitters. Restoration in the late 1980s didn't make the elevators any faster (lines are inevitable), but the nocturnal illumination is fantastic—every girder highlighted in glorious detail. ✉ *quai Branly,* ☎ *01–44–11–23–23.* ✇ *By elevator: 2nd floor, 20 frs; 3rd floor, 40 frs; 4th floor, 56 frs. By foot: 2nd and 3rd floors only, 12 frs.* ☉ *July–Aug., daily 9 AM–midnight; Sept.–June, daily 9 AM–11 PM. Métro: Bir-Hakeim; RER: Champ-de-Mars.*

❿ Grand Palais. With its curved glass roof, the Grand Palais is unmistakable when approached from either the Seine or the Champs-Elysées and forms an attractive duo with the **Petit Palais** on the other side of avenue Winston-Churchill. Both were built for the World Fair of 1900, and, as with the Eiffel Tower, there was never any intention that they would be permanent additions to the city. But once they were up, no one seemed inclined to take them down. Today, the atmospheric iron-and-glass interior of the Grand Palais plays host to major exhibitions but was closed for renovation in 1994 and is unlikely to reopen before 1999. But the Petit Palais contains a permanent collection of French painting and furniture, with splendid canvases by Courbet and Bouguereau. ✉ *av. Winston-Churchill.* ☎ *01–42–65–12–73.* ✇ *27 frs.* ☉ *Tues.–Sun. 10–5:30. Métro: Champs-Elysées–Clemenceau.*

🐣 ⑭ Jardin des Tuileries. The recently renovated Tuileries Gardens are typically French: formal and neatly patterned, with statues, rows of trees, and gravel paths. This is a charming place to stroll and survey the surrounding cityscape. *Métro: Tuileries.*

⑮ Louvre. Though it is now a coherent, unified structure, the Louvre—the world's largest museum—is the product of centuries. Originally built by Philippe-Auguste in the 13th century as a fortress, it was not until the reign of pleasure-loving François I, 300 years later, that today's Louvre gradually began to take shape. Through the years, Henri IV (1589–1610), Louis XIII (1610–43), Louis XIV (1643–1715), Napoléon (1804–14), and Napoléon III (1852–70) all contributed to its construction. Before rampaging revolutionaries burned part of it down during the bloody Paris Commune of 1871, the building was even larger. The open section facing the Tuileries Gardens was originally the

Palais des Tuileries, the main Paris residence of the royal family. In fact, it was from this palace that Louis XVI and Marie-Antoinette fled in 1791, two years after the start of the Revolution, only to be arrested and returned to Paris for their executions.

★ The Louvre's recent history centers on I. M. Pei's glass **Pyramid,** surrounded by three smaller pyramids in the Cour Napoléon. Unveiled in March of 1989, it's more than just a grandiloquent gesture. The pyramid provided a new, and much needed, entrance to the Louvre; it also tops a large museum shop, café, and restaurant. Moreover, it acts as the terminal point for the most celebrated city view in Europe, a majestic vista stretching through the Arc du Carrousel, the Tuileries Gardens, across place de la Concorde, up the Champs-Elysées to the towering Arc de Triomphe, and ending at the giant modern arch at La Défense, 4 km (2½ mi) more to the west. Needless to say, the architectural collision between the classical stone blocks of the courtyard surrounding the pyramid and the pseudo-Egyptian glass panels caused a furor. But, as time has passed, initial outrage has faded—as it once did for the Eiffel Tower.

The pyramids marked only the first phase of the Grand Louvre Project, a plan for the restoration of the museum. In November 1993, exactly 200 years after the Louvre first opened its doors to the public, the second phase was unveiled: the renovation of the **Richelieu wing** on the north side of the Cour Napoléon. The wing contains principally the Islamic and Mesopotamian art collections, French sculpture and painting, and Napoléon III's sumptuous apartments lovingly restored to their full ostentatious glory. The final phase of the Grand Louvre project, which was finished in 1996, included a much-needed improvement of lighting and air-conditioning throughout the museum; on the exterior the remaining facades have been restored and cleaned.

The Louvre's extraordinary collections encompass paintings, drawings, antiquities, sculpture, furniture, coins, and jewelry—the quality and the sheer variety are overwhelming. The number one attraction is Leonardo da Vinci's enigmatic **Mona Lisa,** *La Joconde* to the French. But there are numerous other works of equal quality. The collections are divided into seven areas: Asian antiquities, Egyptian antiquities, Greek and Roman antiquities, sculpture, objets d'art, paintings, and prints and drawings. What follows is no more than a selection of favorites, chosen to act as key points for your exploration. If you have time for only one visit, they give an idea of the riches of the museum. But try to make repeat visits—the Louvre is half price on Sundays and after 3 PM on other days. Study the plans at the entrance to get your bearings and pick up a map to take with you.

French paintings dominate the picture collection. They include: *Embarkation for the Island of Cythera,* by Watteau (1684–1721), which encapsulates the gallant ideal, tinged with melancholy; *Oath of the Horatii,* by David (1748–1825), a purely neoclassical work—severe, uncompromising, and austere; *La Grande Odalisque,* by Ingres (1780–1867), a supremely sensuous yet remote work by this habitually staid "academic" artist; *Liberty Guiding the People,* by Delacroix (1798–1863), which celebrates the courageous spirit of revolutionary idealism, and the *Raft of the "Medusa",* by Géricault (1791–1824), which depicts a nightmarish true event of a raftful of shipwreck survivors.

Although the Mona Lisa tends to dominate the field, the Italian Renaissance is strongly represented by Fra Angelico, Mantegna, Raphael, Titian, and Veronese. Holbein, Van Eyck, Rembrandt, Hals, Brueghel, and Rubens—whose giant Maria de Medici canvases have an entire hall to themselves—underline the achievements of northern European painting. The Spanish painters El Greco, Murillo, and Goya are also represented.

Three-dimensional attractions start with marvels of ancient Greek sculpture, such as the soaring *Victory of Samothrace,* from the 3rd century BC, and the *Venus de Milo,* from the 2nd century BC. One of the best-loved exhibits is Michelangelo's *Slaves,* intended for the unfinished tomb of Pope Julius II. ✉ *Palais du Louvre,* ☎ *01–40–20–53–17 for information.* 🎫 *45 frs; 26 frs after 3 PM and all day Sun.; free 1st Sun. of month.* ☉ *Thurs.–Sun. 9–6, Mon. and Wed. 9 AM–9:45 PM. Some sections open limited days. Métro: Palais-Royal.*

⑤ Musée d'Art Moderne de la Ville de Paris. Both temporary exhibits and the permanent collection of top-quality 20th-century art can be found at the City Museum of Modern Art. Among the earliest works are Fauve paintings by Vlaminck and Derain, followed by Picasso's early experiments in Cubism. Other highlights include works by Braque, Rouault, Gleizes, Da Silva, Gromaire, and Modigliani. There is also a large room devoted to Art Deco furniture and screens, where Jean Dunand's gilt and lacquered panels consume oceans of wall space. ⊠ *11 av. du Président-Wilson,* ☎ *01–53–67–40–00.* ⊡ *27 frs.* ☉ *Tues.–Sun. 10–5:30, Wed. 10–8:30. Métro: Iéna.*

④ Musée Guimet. This Belle Epoque museum was founded by 19th-century Lyonnais industrialist Emile Guimet, who amassed priceless Indo-Chinese and Far Eastern objets d'art. Trouble is, most of the museum is closed for restoration until 1999; just the Heidelbach-Guimet gallery around the corner (⊠ 19 av. d'Iéna), featuring Buddhist art from China and Japan, stays open in the interim. ⊠ *6 pl. d'Iéna,* ☎ *01–47–23–61–65.* ⊡ *15 frs.* ☉ *Wed.–Mon. 9:45–6. Métro: Iéna.*

⑫ Musée du Jeu de Paume. Renovations have transformed this museum into an ultramodern, white-walled showcase for excellent temporary exhibits of bold contemporary art. ⊠ *pl. de la Concorde,* ☎ *01–42–60–69–69.* ⊡ *35 frs.* ☉ *Tues. noon–9:30, Wed.–Fri. noon–7, weekends 10–7. Métro: Concorde.*

⑥ Musée de la Mode et du Costume. The Museum of Fashion and Costume is housed in the stylish, late-19th-century Palais Galliera. Exhibits on costumery and clothing design are held here. ⊠ *10 av. Pierre-1er-de-Serbie,* ☎ *01–47–20–85–23.* ⊡ *26 frs.* ☉ *Tues.–Sun. 10–5:40. Métro: Iéna.*

⑬ Musée de l'Orangerie. Several of Claude Monet's *Water Lily* series head the choice array of early 20th-century paintings in the Orangerie Museum in the Tuileries Gardens. Works by Renoir, Cézanne, Matisse, and Marie Laurencin, the "Popess of Cubism," are also on display. ⊠ *pl. de la Concorde,* ☎ *01–42–97–48.16.* ⊡ *28 frs.* ☉ *Wed.–Mon. 9:45–5:15. Métro: Concorde.*

⑨ Office de Tourisme de la Ville de Paris. The modern, spacious, Paris Tourist Office, near the Arc de Triomphe, is worth a visit at the start of your stay to pick up free maps, leaflets, and information on upcoming events. Most of the uniformed hostesses speak English and can also help book accommodations or tickets for shows. You can also exchange money here and buy métro tickets and souvenirs. ⊠ *127 av. des Champs-Elysées,* ☎ *01–49–52–53–54 (01–49–52–53–56 for recorded information in English).* ☉ *Daily 9–8. Métro: Charles de Gaulle–Etoile.*

③ Palais de Chaillot. This honey-color Art Deco cultural center was built in the 1930s to replace a Moorish-style building constructed for the World Exhibition of 1878. It contains three large museums: the **Musée des Monuments Français** (Museum of French Monuments), whose painstaking replicas of statues and archways form an excellent introduction to French medieval architecture; the **Musée du Cinéma Henri-Langlois** (Cinema Museum), tracing the history of motion pictures; and the **Musée de l'Homme** (Museum of Man), whose array of prehistoric artifacts will serve as the base for a new Primal Art museum to open in 1999. At press time (spring 1997), the **Musée de la Marine** (Maritime Museum), based here for many years, was set to move to an unspecified new location. The tumbling gardens leading to the Seine contain sculptures and some dramatic fountains. ⊠ *pl. du Trocadéro. Métro: Trocadéro.*

⑪ Place de la Concorde. This majestic square at the foot of the Champs-Elysées was laid out in the 1770s, but there was nothing in the way of peace or concord about its early years. Between 1793 and 1795, it was the scene of more than 1,000 deaths by guillotine; victims included Louis XVI, Marie-Antoinette, Danton, and Robespierre. The Obelisk, a present from the viceroy of Egypt, was erected in 1833. At the near end of high-walled rue Royale is the legendary Maxim's restaurant, whose interior is a riot of crimson velvets and florid Art Nouveau furniture. *Métro: Concorde.*

Pont Alexandre-III. No other bridge over the Seine epitomizes the fin de siècle frivolity of the Belle Epoque like the exuberant, bronze lamp-lined Pont Alexandre-III. The bridge was built, like the Grand and Petit Palais nearby, for the 1900 World Fair. *Métro: Invalides.*

THE FAUBOURG ST-HONORÉ

Faubourg St-Honoré—the area just north of the Champs-Elysées and the Tuileries—is synonymous with style, as you will see as you progress from the President's Palace, past a wealth of art galleries and the neo-classical Madeleine church, to stately place Vendôme. Leading names in modern fashion can be found further east on place des Victoires, close to what was, for centuries, the gastronomic heart of Paris: Les Halles (pronounced *lay al*), the city's main produce and meat market. The market halls were closed in 1969 and replaced by a park and a modern shopping mall, the Forum des Halles.

The brash modernity of the Forum stands in contrast to the august church of St-Eustache nearby. Similarly, the incongruous black-and-white columns in the classical courtyard of Richelieu's neighboring Palais-Royal present a further case of daring modernity—or architectural vandalism, depending on your point of view. Parisians may delight in their role as custodians of a glorious heritage, but are not content to remain mere guardians of the past.

Numbers in the margin correspond to numbers on the Faubourg St-Honoré map; these numbers indicate a suggested path for sightseeing.

Sights to See

❽ Bibliothèque Nationale. France's national library used to contain more than 7 million printed volumes; many have been removed to the giant new Bibliothèque François-Mitterrand (☞ The Islands and the Latin Quarter, *below*). You can admire Robert de Cotte's 18th-century courtyard and peep into the magnificent 19th-century reading room, but you cannot enter (it's only open to researchers). ✉ *58 rue de Richelieu.* ☉ *Daily 9–8. Métro: Bourse.*

❻ Comédie Française. This theater is the setting for performances of classical French drama, with tragedies by Racine and Corneille and comedies by Molière regularly on the bill. The building itself dates from 1790, but the Comédie

Française company was created by that most theatrical of French monarchs, Louis XIV, back in 1680. If you understand French and have a taste for the mannered, declamatory style of French acting—it's a far cry from method acting—you'll appreciate an evening here (☞ Theater *in* Chapter 5). ✉ *pl. André-Malraux,* ☎ *01–44–58–15–15. Métro: Palais-Royal.*

② **Église de la Madeleine.** With its rows of uncompromising columns, this sturdy neoclassical edifice—designed in 1814 but not consecrated until 1842—looks more like a Greek temple than a Christian church. In fact, La Madeleine, as it is called, was nearly selected as Paris's first train station (the site of the Gare St-Lazare, just up the road, was chosen instead). The portico's majestic Corinthian colonnade supports a gigantic pediment with a frieze of the Last Judgment. ✉ *pl. de la Madeleine.* ⊙ *Mon.–Sat. 7:30–7, Sun. 8–7. Métro: Madeleine.*

⑪ **Forum des Halles.** Les Halles, the iron-and-glass halls of the central Paris food market, were closed in 1969 and replaced in the late '70s by the Forum des Halles, a modern shopping mall. Nothing remains of either the market or the rambunctious atmosphere that led 19th-century novelist Emile Zola to dub Les Halles *"le ventre de Paris"* ("the belly of Paris"), although rue Montorgueil, behind St-Eustache, retains something of its original bustle. Unfortunately, much of the plastic, concrete, glass, and mock-marble facade of the multilevel shopping mall, still referred to as "Les Halles," is already showing signs of wear and tear. ✉ *Main entrance on rue Pierre-Lescot. Métro or RER: Châtelet–Les Halles.*

⑤ **Musée des Arts Décoratifs.** The Decorative Arts Museum in the Pavillon de Marsan, the northwestern wing of the Louvre, houses more than 50,000 objects charting the course of French furniture and applied arts through the centuries. ✉ *107 rue de Rivoli.* 💳 *20 frs.* ⊙ *Wed.–Sat. 12:30– 6, Sun. noon–6. Métro: Palais-Royal.*

① **Palais de l'Elysée.** This "palace," where the French president lives, works, and receives official visitors, was originally constructed as a private mansion in 1718. The Elysée has housed presidents only since 1873; before then, Madame

The Faubourg St-Honoré

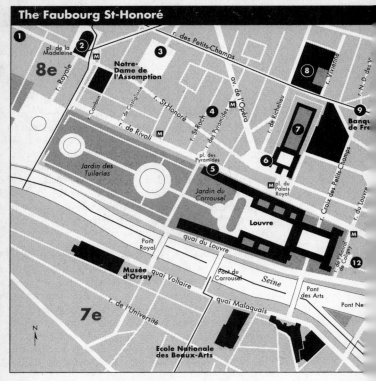

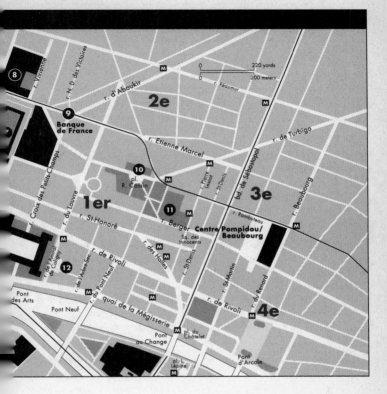

de Pompadour (Louis XV's influential mistress), Napoléon, Josephine, the Duke of Wellington, and Queen Victoria all stayed here. The building is closed to the public. ⊠ *55 rue du Faubourg-St-Honoré. Métro: Miromesnil.*

⑦ Palais-Royal. The buildings of this former palace—royal only in that all-powerful Cardinal Richelieu (1585–1642) magnanimously bequeathed them to Louis XIII—date from the 1630s. Today, the Palais-Royal is home to the French Ministry of Culture, and its buildings are not open to the public. They overlook a colonnaded courtyard with black-and-white striped half-columns and revolving silver spheres that slither around in two fountains, the controversial work of architect Daniel Buren. The splendid gardens beyond are bordered by arcades harboring discreet boutiques and divided by rows of perfectly trimmed little trees. ⊠ *pl. du Palais-Royal. Métro: Palais-Royal.*

⑨ Place des Victoires. This circular square, now home to many of the city's top fashion boutiques, was laid out in 1685 by Jules-Hardouin Mansart in honor of the military victories of Louis XIV, that indefatigable warrior whose nearly continuous battles may have brought much prestige to his country but came perilously close to bringing it to bankruptcy, too. Louis is shown galloping along on a bronze horse in the middle. *Métro: Sentier.*

③ Place Vendôme. With its granite pavement and Second Empire street lamps, Mansart's rhythmic, perfectly proportioned example of 17th-century urban architecture shines in all its golden-stoned splendor. Napoléon had the square's central column made from the melted bronze of 1,200 cannons captured at the battle of Austerlitz in 1805. That's him standing vigilantly at the top. Painter Gustave Courbet headed the Revolutionary hooligans who, in 1871, toppled the column and shattered it into thousands of metallic pieces. The Third Republic stuck them together again and sent him the bill. There's parking in an underground lot. *Métro: Opéra.*

⑩ St-Eustache. Since the demolition of the 19th-century iron-and-glass market halls at the beginning of the '70s, St-Eustache has reemerged as a dominant element on the central Paris skyline. It is a huge church, the "cathedral" of Les

Halles, built as the market people's Right Bank reply to Notre-Dame on the Ile de la Cité. With the exception of the feeble west front, added between 1754 and 1788, construction lasted from 1532 to 1637, spanning the decline of the Gothic style and the emergence of the Renaissance. As a consequence, the church is a curious architectural hybrid. Its exterior flying buttresses are Gothic, but its column orders, rounded arches, and thick, comparatively simple window tracery are unmistakably classical. ⊠ *2 rue du Jour,* ☏ *01–46–27–89–21 for concert information.* ☉ *Daily 8–7. Métro or RER: Châtelet–Les Halles.*

⑫ **St-Germain l'Auxerrois.** Until 1789, this was used by the French royal family as their Paris parish church, in the days when the adjacent Louvre was a palace rather than a museum. The fluid stonework of the facade reveals the influence of 15th-century Flamboyant Gothic style, enjoying its final neurotic shrieks before the classical takeover of the Renaissance. Notice the unusually wide windows in the nave and the equally unusual double aisles. ⊠ *pl. du Louvre. Métro: Louvre-Rivoli.*

❹ **St-Roch.** This huge church, designed by Lemercier in 1653 but completed only in the 1730s, is almost as long as Notre-Dame (138 yards) thanks to Hardouin-Mansart's domed Lady Chapel at the far end, with its elaborate Baroque altarpiece. Classical playwright Pierre Corneille (1606–84) is buried here; a commemorative plaque honors him at the left of the entrance. ⊠ *rue St-Honoré. Métro: Tuileries.*

THE GRAND BOULEVARDS

The focal point of this area is the uninterrupted avenue that runs in almost a straight line from St-Augustin, the city's grandest Second Empire church, to place de la République, whose very name symbolizes the ultimate downfall of the imperial regime. The avenue's name changes six times along the way, which is why Parisians refer to it, in plural, as the Grands Boulevards.

The makeup of the neighborhoods along the Grand Boulevards changes steadily as you head east from the posh 8ᵉ arrondissement toward working-class east Paris. The *grands magasins* (department stores), such as Au Printemps and Galeries Lafayette, epitomize upscale Paris shopping; these are found on Boulevard Haussmann, named in honor of the regional prefect who oversaw the reconstruction of the city in the 1850s and 1860s. The opulent Opéra Garnier, just past the *grands magasins,* is the architectural showpiece of the period (often termed the Second Empire and corresponding to the rule of Napoléon III).

Haussmann's concept of urban planning proved grand enough to ward off the postwar skyscrapers and property sharks that bedevil so many other European cities (Paris's urban planners relegated them to the outskirts of the city). Though the boulevards are lined with the seven-story blocks typical of Haussmann's time, they date from the 1670s, when the streets were created on the site of the city's medieval fortifications. These were razed when Louis XIV's military triumphs appeared to render their raison d'être obsolete, and replaced by leafy promenades known from the outset as "boulevards."

Numbers in the margin correspond to numbers on the Grand Boulevards map; these numbers indicate a suggested path for sightseeing.

Sights to See

⑧ Bourse. The Paris Stock Exchange, a serene, colonnaded 19th-century building, is a far cry from Wall Street. Take your passport if you want to tour it. ✉ *rue Vivienne.* 🎫 *30 frs. Guided tours only (in French), weekdays every ½ hr 1:15–4. Métro: Bourse.*

⑭ Canal St-Martin. Place de la République is the gateway to east Paris, a largely residential area often underestimated by tourists. One of its highlights is the Canal St-Martin, which starts just south of place de la Bastille but really comes into its own during the mile-long stretch north of République across the 10ᵉ arrondissement. The canal was originally built at the behest of Napoléon, with the aim of providing the city with drinking water. With its quiet banks, locks, and footbridges, the canal is much-loved by novelists and film directors; Simenon's famous inspector Maigret solved many a mystery along its deceptively sleepy banks. *Métro: Jacques-Bonsergent, Jaurès.*

25

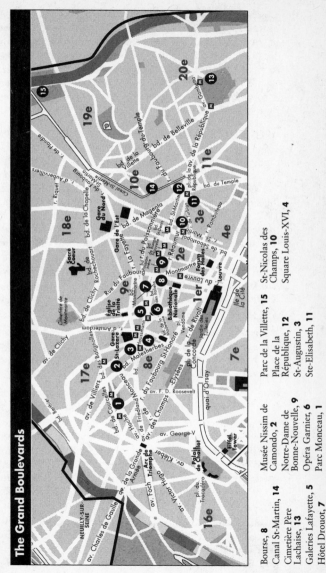

The Grand Boulevards

Bourse, **8**
Canal St-Martin, **14**
Cimetière Père
Lachaise, **13**
Galeries Lafayette, **5**
Hôtel Drouot, **7**

Musée Nissim de
Camondo, **2**
Notre-Dame de
Bonne-Nouvelle, **9**
Opéra Garnier, **6**
Parc Monceau, **1**

Parc de la Villette, **15**
Place de la
République, **12**
St-Augustin, **3**
Ste-Elisabeth, **11**

St-Nicolas des
Champs, **10**
Square Louis-XVI, **4**

25

⓭ **Cimetière Père Lachaise.** The largest, most interesting, and
most prestigious of Paris's cemeteries dates from the start
of the 19th century. On the eastern fringe of Paris, it is a
veritable necropolis whose tombs compete in grandiosity,
originality, and often, alas, dilapidation. Cobbled avenues,
steep slopes, and lush vegetation create a powerful atmosphere. The cemetery houses the tombs of the French author Colette; the composer Chopin; the playwright Molière;
the writers Honoré Balzac, Marcel Proust, Paul Eluard, Oscar
Wilde, and Gertrude Stein; the popular French actress Simone Signoret and her husband, singer-actor Yves Mon-
tand; and Edith Piaf. Perhaps the most noticeable shrine is
to rock star Jim Morrison, where dozens of faithful come
to pay homage to the songwriter. The cemetery was also
the site of the Paris Commune's final battle, on May 28,
1871, when the rebel troops were rounded up, lined against
the Mur des Fédérés (Federalists' Wall) in the southeast corner, and shot. Get hold of a map at the entrance—Père
Lachaise is an easy place to get lost in. ✉ *Entrances on rue
des Rondeaux, bd. de Ménilmontant, and rue de la Réunion.*
☉ *Daily 8–6; winter, daily 8–dusk. Métro: Gambetta,
Philippe-Auguste, Père Lachaise.*

⓹ **Galeries Lafayette.** This turn-of-the-century department
store has a vast, shimmering, Belle Epoque glass dome that
can only be seen if you venture inside. (☞ Department Stores
in Chapter 6). ✉ *40 bd. Haussmann. Métro: Chaussée
d'Antin; RER: Auber.*

⓻ **Hôtel Drouot.** Hidden away in a grid of narrow streets not
far from the Opéra is Paris's central auction house, offering everything from stamps and toy soldiers to Renoirs and
18th-century commodes. The 16 salesrooms make for fascinating browsing, and there's no obligation to bid. Sales
are held most weekdays, with viewings in the morning; anyone can attend. ✉ *9 rue Drouot,* ☎ *01–48–00–20–00.*
☉ *Viewings Mon.–Sat. 11–noon and 2–6, with auctions
starting at 2. Métro: Richelieu-Drouot.*

⓶ **Musée Nissim de Camondo.** The elegant decadence of the
last days of the regal Ancien Régime (1770–90) is fully reflected in the lavish interior of this aristocratic Parisian mansion, built in the style of Louis XVI. ✉ *63 rue de Monceau,*

☎ 01–45–63–26–32. 🎫 27 frs. ☉ Wed.–Sun. 10–noon and 2–5. Métro: Monceau.

❾ Notre-Dame de Bonne-Nouvelle. This wide, soberly neo-classical church is tucked away off the Grand Boulevards. As you approach it, you'll see the crooked church tower, surrounded by rickety housing that looks straight out of Balzac. ⊠ rue de la Lune. Métro: Bonne-Nouvelle.

❻ Opéra Garnier. From an architectural standpoint, the original Paris Opera, begun in 1862 by Charles Garnier at the behest of Napoléon III, has as much subtlety as the crash of cymbals. After paying the entry fee, you can stroll around at leisure. The monumental foyer and staircase are impressive—a stage in their own right. If the lavishly upholstered auditorium seems small, it is only because the stage is the largest in the world—more than 11,000 square yards, with room for up to 450 performers. Marc Chagall painted the ceiling in 1964. ⊠ pl. de l'Opéra, ☎ 01–40–01–22–63. 🎫 30 frs. ☉ Daily 10–4:30; closed occasionally for rehearsals; call 01–47–42–57–50 to check. Métro: Opéra.

🍼 ❶ Parc Monceau. The most picturesque gardens on the Right Bank were laid out as a private park in 1778 and retain some of the fanciful elements then in vogue, including mock ruins and a phony pyramid. ⊠ Entrances on bd. de Courcelles, av. Velasquez, av. Ruysdaël, av. van Dyck. Métro: Monceau.

🍼 ❶❺ Parc de la Villette. Until the 1970s this 130-acre site, in an unfashionable corner of northeast Paris commonly known as "La Villette," was home to a cattle market and slaughterhouse (abattoir). Only the slaughterhouse, known as **La Grande Halle,** remains: a magnificent iron-and-glass structure ingeniously transformed into an exhibition-cum-con-cert center. But everything else here—from the science museum and spherical cinema to the music academy, each interconnected by designer gardens—is futuristic. The complex was finished in 1997 with the **Cité de la Musique** (☞ Chapter 5), a giant postmodern musical academy with a state-of-the-art concert hall and a spectacular museum of musical instruments, the **Musée de la Musique.** The museum contains a mind-tingling array of 900 instruments that sound as you pass thanks to infrared headphones. ⊠ 221 *av. Jean-Jaurès,* ☎ *01–44–84–46–21.* ⌺ *Music Museum 35 frs.* ☉ *Tues.–Thurs. noon–6, Fri. noon–9:30, Sat. noon–6, Sun. 10–6. Métro: Porte de Pantin.*

The pompously styled **Cité des Sciences et de l'Industrie** tries to do for science and industry what the Pompidou Center does for modern art. The brave attempt to render technology fun and easy involves dozens of try-it-yourself contraptions that make you feel more participant than onlooker. ⌧ *30 av. Corentin-Cariou,* ☎ *08–36–68–29–30.* ⌺ *50 frs (planetarium 25 frs), 25 frs after 4PM.* ☉ *Wed.–Sun. 10– noon and 2–6. Métro: Porte de la Villette.*

⓬ **Place de la République.** This large, oblong square, laid out by Haussmann in 1856–65, is dominated by a matronly, Stalin-size statue symbolizing *The Republic* (1883). The square is often used as a rallying point for demonstrations. *Métro: République.*

❸ **St-Augustin.** This domed church was dexterously constructed in the 1860s within the confines of an awkward, V-shape site. It represented a breakthrough in ecclesiastical engineering, insofar as the use of metal pillars and girders obviated the need for exterior buttressing. ⌧ *pl. St-Augustin. Métro: St-Augustin.*

⓫ **Ste-Elisabeth.** This studied essay in Baroque (1628–46) is pleasantly unpretentious; there's no soaring bombast here. The church has a stupendous 17th-century wood panel transferred from an abbey at Arras in northern France. ⌧ *rue du Temple. Métro: Temple.*

❿ **St-Nicolas des Champs.** The rounded-arch, fluted Doric capitals in the chancel of this church date from 1560 to 1587, a full century later than the pointed-arch nave (1420–80). ⌧ *rue St-Martin. Métro: Arts et Métiers.*

❹ **Square Louis-XVI.** An unkempt mausoleum emerges defiantly from the lush undergrowth of this verdant square off boulevard Haussmann, marking the initial burial site of Louis XVI and Marie-Antoinette after their turns at the guillotine on place de la Concorde. Two stone tablets are inscribed with the last missives of the doomed royals: touching pleas for their Revolutionary enemies to be forgiven. ☉ *Daily 10– noon and 2–6; winter, daily 10–4. Métro: St-Augustin.*

THE MARAIS AND THE BASTILLE

The Marais is one of Paris's oldest, most historic, and sought-after residential districts. Renovation is the keynote; well into the '70s this was filled with dilapidated tenements and squalid courtyards. The area's regeneration was sparked by the building of the Centre Pompidou (known to Parisians as Beaubourg), arguably Europe's most architecturally whimsical museum. The gracious architecture of the 17th and early 18th centuries, however, sets the tone for the rest of the Marais. Today, most of the Marais's spectacular *hôtels particuliers*—loosely, "mansions," onetime residences of aristocratic families—have been restored and many are now museums. There are trendy boutiques and cafés among the kosher shops in the formerly run-down streets of the Jewish neighborhood around rue des Rosiers.

On the eastern edge of the Marais, in the Bastille neighborhood, is place de la Bastille, site of the infamous prison stormed on July 14, 1789: an event that came to symbolize the beginning of the French Revolution. Largely in commemoration of the bicentennial of the Revolution, the Bastille area was renovated and became one of the trendiest sections of Paris.

Numbers in the margin correspond to numbers on the Marais and the Bastille map; these numbers indicate a suggested path for sightseeing.

Sights to See

 Archives Nationales. If you're a serious history buff, you will be fascinated by the thousands of intricate historical documents, dating from the Merovingian period to the 20th century, at the National Archives (also known as the Musée de l'Histoire de France) in the palatial Hôtel de Soubise. The highlights are the Edict of Nantes (1598), the Treaty of Westphalia (1648), the wills of Louis XIV and Napoléon, and the Declaration of Human Rights (1789). Louis XVI's diary is also in the collection, containing his sadly ignorant entry for July 14, 1789, the day the Bastille was stormed and, for all intents and purposes, the French Revolution began: "*Rien*" ("Nothing"). ⊠ *60 rue des Francs-Bourgeois,* ☏ *01-40-27-62-18.* ▨ *15 frs.* ☉ *Wed.–Mon. 1:45–5:45. Métro: Rambuteau.*

The Marais and the Bastille

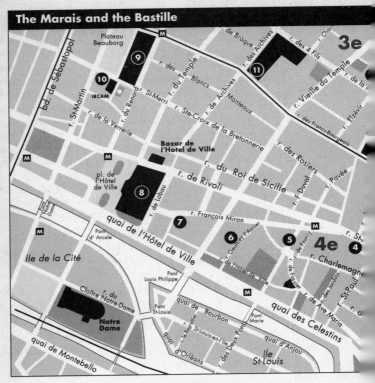

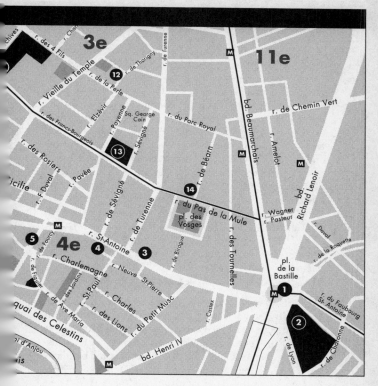

⑨ Centre Pompidou. The Centre National d'Art et de Culture Georges-Pompidou is its full name, although it is known to Parisians simply as Beaubourg (for the district). Unveiled in 1977, the Pompidou Center was soon attracting over 8 million visitors a year—five times more than intended. Hardly surprising, then, that it was soon showing signs of fatigue: The much-vaunted, gaudily painted service pipes snaking up the exterior needed continual repainting, while the plastic tubing enclosing the exterior escalators was cracked and grimy. In 1996 the government stepped in and took drastic action: shutting the Center until December 1999 and embarking on top-to-bottom renovation. It's still worth passing by, of course. Although the Center is closed, the escalator up to the roof remains open, with the Parisian skyline unfolding as you are carried through the clear plastic tubes. Inside, some exhibitions will be staged when restoration allows. ⊠ *pl. Georges-Pompidou,* ☎ *01–44–78–12–33.* ▥ *Building and library entry and escalator ride to the roof: free. Exhibitions: prices vary, check at the main ticket booth on the ground floor.* ⊙ *Wed.–Mon. noon–10, weekends 10–10; closed Tues. Métro: Rambuteau.*

❸ Hôtel de Sully. This late-Renaissance mansion, begun in 1624, has a stately garden and a majestic courtyard. It is the headquarters of the **Caisse Nationale des Monuments Historiques,** responsible for administering France's historic monuments. Guided visits to Paris sites and buildings begin here, though all are conducted in French. ⊠ *62 rue St-Antoine,* ☎ *01–44–61–20–00. Métro: St-Paul.*

❽ Hôtel de Ville. The City Hall, overlooking the Seine, is something of a symbol for the regeneration of the surrounding Marais district, since much of the finance and direction for the restoration of the area has been provided by municipal authorities. Today's exuberant building went up between 1874 and 1884; it's based closely on the 16th-century Renaissance original, which was burned during the Commune of 1871. The square in front was once the site of public executions; here, Robespierre, the fanatical Revolutionary, came to suffer the fate of his many victims when a furious mob accompanied him to the guillotine in 1794. ⊠ *pl. de l'Hôtel-de-Ville.* ⊙ *For special exhibitions. Métro: Hôtel-de-Ville.*

⑤ Maison Européenne de la Photographie. This beautiful museum, unveiled in 1996, is housed in two hôtels particuliers. Despite its name, the museum has an impressive collection of both European and American works. ⊠ *5 rue Fourcy,* ☎ *01–44–78–75–00.* ☜ *30 frs. Free Wed. after 5 PM.* ☉ *Wed.–Sun. 11–8. Métro: St-Paul.*

⑥ Mémorial du Martyr Inconnu. In March 1992, this Memorial of the Unknown Jewish Martyr was erected at the **Center for Contemporary Jewish Documentation**—50 years after the first convoy of deportees left France—to honor the memory of the 6 million Jews who died "without graves." The basement crypt has a dramatic, black marble Star of David containing the ashes of victims from Nazi death camps in Poland and Austria. The center has archives, a library, and a gallery that hosts temporary exhibitions. ⊠ *17 rue Geoffroy-l'Asnier,* ☎ *01–42–77–44–72.* ☜ *12 frs.* ☉ *Sun.–Fri. 10–1 and 2–6. Métro: Pont-Marie.*

⑬ Musée Carnavalet. Two adjacent mansions in the heart of the Marais house the Carnavelet Museum, the Paris History Museum. Material dating from the city's origins until 1789 is in the Hôtel Carnavalet, and material from 1789 to the present is in the Hôtel Peletier St-Fargeau. The Hôtel Carnavalet, transformed into a museum in 1880, is full of maps and plans, furniture, and busts and portraits of Parisian worthies down the ages. The section on the Revolution includes riveting models of guillotines and objects associated with the royal family's final days, including the king's razor, and the chess set used by the royal prisoners at the approach of their own endgame. ⊠ *23 rue de Sévigné,* ☎ *01–42–72–21–13.* ☜ *27 frs.* ☉ *Tues.–Sun. 10–5:30. Métro: St-Paul.*

⑫ Musée Picasso. The Picasso Museum opened in the fall of 1985 and shows no signs of losing its immense popularity. It's the largest collection of works by Picasso in the world—no masterpieces, but all works kept by Picasso himself; in other words, works that he especially valued. There are pictures from every period of his life: a grand total of 230 paintings, 1,500 drawings, and nearly 1,700 prints, as well as works by Cézanne, Miró, Renoir, Braque, Degas, and Matisse. The palatial surroundings of the 17th-century Hôtel Salé (literally, salted) add to the pleasures of a visit. ⊠ *5* *rue de Thorigny,* ☎ *01–42–71–25–21.* 📧 *28 frs, Sun. 18 frs.* ☉ *Thurs.–Mon. 9:30–6. Métro: St-Sébastien.*

② Opéra de la Bastille. The state-of-the-art Bastille Opera was erected on the south side of place de la Bastille. Designed by Argentine-born Carlos Ott, it opened July 14, 1989, the bicentennial of the French Revolution. The steep-climbing auditorium seats more than 3,000 and has earned more plaudits than the curving glass facade, which strikes Parisians as depressingly like that of yet another modern office building. ✉ *pl. de la Bastille,* ☎ *01–44–73–13–00. Métro: Bastille.*

① Place de la Bastille. Nothing remains of the infamous Bastille prison destroyed at the beginning of the French Revolution. Until 1988, there was little more to see here than a huge traffic circle and the **Colonne de Juillet,** the July Column. As part of the countrywide celebrations for July 1989, the bicentennial of the French Revolution, the Opéra de la Bastille was erected, inspiring substantial redevelopment on the surrounding streets, especially along rue de Lappe—once a haunt of Edith Piaf—and rue de la Roquette. What was formerly a humdrum neighborhood rapidly became one of the most sparkling and attractive in the city. Streamlined art galleries, funky jazz clubs, and Spanish-style tapas bars set the tone.

The Bastille, or, more properly, the Bastille St-Antoine, was a massive building; its ground plan is marked by paving stones set into the modern square. It was used almost exclusively to house political prisoners—Voltaire, the Marquis de Sade, and the mysterious Man in the Iron Mask were all incarcerated here, along with many other unfortunates. It was this obviously political role—specifically, the fact that the prisoners were nearly always held by order of the king—that led the "furious mob" (in all probability no more than a largely unarmed rabble) to break into the prison on July 14, 1789, kill the governor, steal what firearms they could find, and free the seven remaining prisoners. Later in 1789, the prison was knocked down. *Métro: Bastille.*

⑭ Place des Vosges. Laid out by Henri IV at the start of the 17th century, this square is the oldest in Paris. It was always a highly desirable address, reaching a peak of glamour in the early years of Louis XIV's reign, when the nobility were falling over themselves for the privilege of living here. The two larger buildings on either side of the square were originally the king's and queen's pavilions. At No. 6 is the Maison de Victor Hugo, where the workaholic French author, famed for *Les Misérables* and *The Hunchback of Notre-Dame*, lived between 1832 and 1848. ⊠ *Maison de Victor Hugo, 6 pl. des Vosges,* ☎ *01–42–72–10–16.* ☎ *27 frs.* ☉ *Tues.–Sun. 10–5:45. Métro: St-Paul, Chemin-Vert.*

❼ St-Gervais–St-Protais. This imposing church is a riot of Flamboyant-style decoration; it went up between 1494 and 1598, making it one of the last Gothic constructions in the country. Pause to look at the 17th-century facade, an early example of French architects' use of the classical orders of decoration on the capitals (topmost sections) of the columns. Those on the first floor are plain and sturdy Doric; the more elaborate Ionic is used on the second floor; and the most ornate of all—Corinthian—is used on the third floor. ⊠ *pl. St-Gervais,* ☎ *01–47–26–78–38 for concert information.* ☉ *Tues.–Sun. 6:30 AM–8 PM. Métro: Hôtel-de-Ville.*

❹ St-Paul–St-Louis. The leading Baroque church in the Marais was begun in 1627 by the Jesuits and partly modeled on their Gesu church in Rome. Look out for Delacroix's dramatic *Christ in the Mount of Olives* high up in the transept, and the two huge shells, used as fonts, presented by Victor Hugo when he lived on nearby place des Vosges. ⊠ *rue St-Antoine. Métro: St-Paul.*

❿ Square Igor-Stravinsky. The café-lined square, around the corner from the Pompidou Center, has a fountain animated by the colorful and imaginative sculptures of French artist Niki de St-Phalle, together with the aquatic mechanisms of Jean Tinguely. It's not exactly part of the Pompidou Center, but it fits in. *Métro: Rambuteau.*

THE ISLANDS AND THE LATIN QUARTER

Of the two islands in the Seine—the Ile St-Louis and the Ile de la Cité—it is the Ile de la Cité that forms the historic heart of Paris. It was here that the earliest inhabitants of Paris, the Gaulish tribe of the Parisii, settled in about 250 BC. Whereas the Ile St-Louis is today largely residential, the Ile de la Cité remains deeply historic. It has been inhabited for more than 2,000 years and is the site of one of the most beautiful churches in France—the great, brooding cathedral of Notre-Dame. Most of the island's other medieval buildings fell victim to town planner Baron Haussmann's ambitious rebuilding program of the 1860s. Among the rare survivors are the jewel-like Ste-Chapelle, a vision of shimmering stained glass, and the Conciergerie, the former city prison.

South of Ile de la Cité on the Left Bank of the Seine is the bohemian Quartier Latin, with its warren of steep sloping streets, populated largely by Sorbonne students and academics who fill the air of the cafés with their ideas—and tobacco smoke. The name Latin Quarter comes from the university tradition of studying and speaking in Latin, a tradition that disappeared during the Revolution.

Numbers in the margin correspond to numbers on the Islands and the Latin Quarter map; these numbers indicate a suggested path for sightseeing.

Sights to See

⑭ Arènes de Lutèce. This Roman arena was only discovered in 1869 and has since been excavated and landscaped to reveal parts of the original amphitheater. You can still see part of the stage and tiered seating. Along with the remains of the baths at the Cluny, this constitutes rare evidence of the powerful Roman city of Lutetia that flourished on the Left Bank in the 3rd century. ⊠ *Enter by rue Monge or rue de Navarre.* ☉ *Daily 8–sunset. Métro: Monge.*

⑬ Bibliothèque François Mitterrand. As the last of former president Mitterrand's *grands travaux* (grand building projects), the *Très Grande Bibliothèque* (Very Big Library, as some facetiously call it) opened in early 1997. The new library subsumes the majority of the collections in the old Bibliothèque Nationale and, with some 11 million volumes between its walls, surpasses the Library of Congress as the largest library in the world. ⊠ *11 quai François-Mauriac,* ☎ *01–53–79–53–79. Métro: Quai de la Gare.*

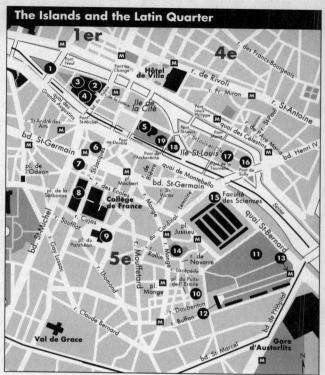

The Islands and the Latin Quarter

② Conciergerie. This turreted medieval building by the Seine
was originally part of the royal palace on Ile de la Cité. Most
people know it, however, as a prison, the place of con-
finement for Danton, Robespierre, and, most famously,
Marie-Antoinette during the French Revolution. From here,
all three—and countless others who fell foul of the Revolutionary leaders—were bundled off to the guillotine. Marie-
Antoinette's cell can still be seen, as well as objects connected
with the ill-fated queen. ⊠ *Entrance on quai de l'Horloge.*
🎫 *28 frs.* ☉ *Daily 9:30–6:30; winter, daily 10–5. Métro:*
Cité.

⊙ ⑫ Grande Galerie de l'Evolution. This vast, handsome glass-
and-iron structure in the Jardin des Plantes (☞ *below*) was
built, as was the Eiffel Tower, in 1889 but abandoned in
the 1960s. It reopened amid popular acclaim in 1994 and
now contains one of the world's finest collections of stuffed
animals, including a section devoted to extinct and en-
dangered species. Stunning lighting effects include a roof
that changes color to suggest storms, twilight, or hot sa-
vannah sun. ⊠ *36 rue Geoffroy-St-Hilaire,* ☏ *01–40–79–*
39–39. 🎫 *40 frs, 30 frs before 1 PM.* ☉ *Wed.–Mon. 10–6,*
Thurs. 10–10. Métro: Monge.

⑯ Ile St-Louis. The smaller of the two Paris islands is linked
to the Ile de la Cité by Pont St-Louis. The contrast between
the islands is striking: Whereas the Ile de la Cité is steeped
in history and dotted with dignified public buildings, the
Ile St-Louis is a discreet residential district. The island's most
striking feature is its architectural unity, which stems from
the efforts of a group of early 17th-century property spec-
ulators, who commissioned leading Baroque architect Louis
Le Vau (1612–70) to erect a series of imposing town
houses. People still talk about the quaint, village-street feel
of rue St-Louis-en-l'Ile, which runs the length of the island,
bisecting it neatly in two. *Métro: Pont-Marie.*

⑮ Institut du Monde Arabe. Jean Nouvel's striking glass-and-
steel edifice, the Institute of the Arab World, adroitly fuses
Arabic and European styles and was greeted with enthusiasm when it opened in 1988. Note the 240 shutterlike
apertures that open and close to regulate light exposure.
Inside, the Institute tries to do for Arab culture what
Beaubourg does for modern art, with the help of a sound-

In case you're running low.

We're here to help with more than 118,000 Express Cash locations around the world. In order to enroll, just call American Express before you start your vacation.

do more

AMERICAN
EXPRESS

Express Cash

And just in case.

We're here with American Express® Travelers Cheques and Cheques *for Two*.® They're the safest way to carry money on your vacation and the surest way to get a refund, practically anywhere, anytime.
Another way we help you...

do more.®

AMERICAN EXPRESS

Travelers Cheques

and-image center; a vast library and documentation center; and an art museum containing an array of Arab-Islamic art. ⊠ *1 rue des Fossés-St-Bernard,* ☎ *01–40–51–38–38.* 🎟 *25 frs.* ☉ *Tues.–Sun. 10–6. Métro: Cardinal-Lemoine.*

🖐 ⑪ **Jardin des Plantes.** Bordered by the Seine, this enormous swath of greenery contains botanical gardens, the Grande Galerie de l'Evolution, and three other natural history museums. The **Grande Galerie de l'Evolution** (☞ *above*) is devoted to stuffed animals; the **Musée Entomologique** to insects; the **Musée Paléontologique** to fossils and prehistoric animals; and the **Musée Minéralogique** to rocks and minerals. The garden is claimed to shelter Paris's oldest tree, an *acacia robinia,* planted in 1636. ⊠ *Entrances on rue Geoffroy-St-Hilaire, rue Buffon.* 🎟 *Museums and zoo 12– 25 frs.* ☉ *Museums Mon. and Wed.–Fri. 9–11:45 and 1– 4:45, weekends 2–4:45; garden daily 7:30* AM*–sunset. Métro: Monge.*

⑱ **Mémorial de la Déportation.** On the eastern tip of the Ile de la Cité, in what was once the city morgue, lies a starkly moving modern crypt, dedicated to those French men, women, and children who died in Nazi concentration camps. 🎟 *Free.* ☉ *Daily 9–6; winter, daily 9–dusk. Métro: Maubert-Mutualité.*

⑩ **Mosquée.** This beautiful white mosque was built from 1922 to 1925, complete with arcades and minaret, and decorated in the style of Moorish Spain. The sunken garden and tiled patios are open to the public (the prayer rooms are not) and so are the *hammams,* or Turkish baths. ⊠ *2 pl. du Puits-de-l'Ermite,* ☎ *01–45–35–97–33.* 🎟 *15 frs for guided tour, 65 frs for Turkish baths.* ☉ *Baths daily 11–8; Fri. and Sun. men only; Mon., Wed., Thurs., and Sat. women only. Guided tours of mosque Sat.–Thurs. 10– noon and 2–5:30. Métro: Monge.*

⑦ **Musée National du Moyen-Age.** The National Museum of the Middle Ages is housed in the 15th-century Hôtel de Cluny. The mansion has an intricately vaulted chapel and a cloistered courtyard; a stunning array of tapestries heads its vast exhibition of medieval decorative arts, including the graceful *Dame à la Licorne* (Lady and the Unicorn), woven in the 15th or 16th century, probably in the southern

Netherlands. Alongside the mansion are the city's two Roman baths, one containing the *Boatmen's Pillar,* Paris's oldest sculpture. ⊠ *6 pl. Paul-Painlevé,* ☎ *01–43–25–62–00.* ▣ *28 frs, Sun. 18 frs.* ⊙ *Wed.–Mon. 9:45–5:45. Métro: Cluny–La Sorbonne.*

★ ❺ **Notre-Dame.** Looming above the large, pedestrian place du Parvis on the Ile de la Cité is the Cathédrale de Notre-Dame, the most enduring symbol of Paris. The square (*kilomètre zéro* to the French, the spot from which all distances to and from the city are officially measured) is the perfect place to assess the facade. The cathedral was begun in 1163, with an army of stonemasons, carpenters, and sculptors working on a site that had previously seen a Roman temple, an early Christian basilica, and a Romanesque church. The chancel and altar were consecrated in 1182, but the magnificent sculptures surrounding the main doors were not put into position until 1240.

Despite various changes in the 17th century, principally the removal of the rose windows, the cathedral remained substantially unaltered until the French Revolution. Then, the statues of the kings of Israel were hacked down by the mob, chiefly because they were thought to represent the despised royal line of France, and everything inside and out that was deemed "anti-Republican" was stripped away. By the early 19th century, the excesses of the Revolution were over, and the cathedral went back to fulfilling its religious functions again. Napoléon crowned himself emperor here in May 1804 (David's heroic painting of the lavish ceremony can be seen in the Louvre). Full-scale restoration started in the middle of the century, the most conspicuous result of which was the reconstruction of the spire. It was then, too, that Haussmann demolished the warren of little buildings in front of the cathedral, creating place du Parvis.

The facade divides neatly into three levels. At the first-floor level are the three main entrances, or portals: the Portal of the Virgin on the left, the Portal of the Last Judgment in the center, and the Portal of St. Anne on the right. Above these are the restored statues of the kings of Israel, the Galerie des Rois. Above the gallery is the great rose window and, above that, the Grand Galerie, at the base of the twin towers. The 387-step climb to the top of the towers is worth the effort for a close-up of the famous gargoyles—most of them added in the 19th century—and the expansive view of the city.

The cathedral interior, with its vast proportions, soaring nave, and soft, multicolor light filtering through the stained-glass windows, inspires awe, despite the inevitable throngs of tourists. Visit early in the morning, when the cathedral is at its lightest and least crowded. On the south side of the chancel is the **Trésor** (treasury), with a collection of garments, reliquaries, and silver and gold plate. ⊠ *pl. du Parvis.* ▣ *Tower 28 frs; treasury 15 frs.* ☉ *Cathedral 8–7; tower daily (summer) 9:30–12:15 and 2–6, daily (winter) 10–5; treasury weekdays 9:30–6. Métro: Cité.*

❸ **Palais de Justice.** The city Law Courts were built by Baron Haussmann in his characteristically weighty neoclassical style in about 1860. You can wander around the buildings, watch the bustle of the lawyers, or attend a court hearing. But the real interest here is the medieval part of the complex, spared by Haussmann: the Conciergerie and Ste-Chapelle (☞ *above* and *below*). ⊠ *bd. du Palais. Métro: Cité.*

❾ **Panthéon.** Originally commissioned as a church by Louis XV, as a mark of gratitude for his recovery from a grave illness in 1744, the Panthéon is now a monument to France's most glorious historical figures. The crypt holds the remains of Voltaire, Zola, Rousseau, and dozens of French statesmen, military heroes, and other thinkers. ⊠ *pl. du Panthéon,* ☎ *01–43–54–34–51.* ▣ *32 frs.* ☉ *Daily 10–5:30. Métro: Cardinal-Lemoine; RER: Luxembourg.*

❿ **Pont de l'Archevêché.** This bridge, built in 1828, links Ile St-Louis to the Left Bank. The bridge offers a breathtaking view of the east end of the cathedral, ringed by flying buttresses, floating above the Seine like some vast stone ship. *Métro: Maubert-Mutualité.*

❶ **Pont Neuf.** Crossing the Ile de la Cité, just behind square du Vert-Galant, is the oldest bridge in Paris, confusingly called the New Bridge, or Pont Neuf. It was completed in 1607 and was the first bridge in the city to be built without houses lining either side. *Métro: Pont-Neuf.*

★ **❹** **Ste-Chapelle.** The Holy Chapel built by the genial and pious Louis IX (1226–70) was conceived as home for what Louis believed to be the crown of thorns from Christ's crucifixion and fragments of the true cross; he acquired these from the impoverished Emperor Baldwin of Constantinople at phenomenal expense. Architecturally, for all its delicate and ornate exterior decoration—notice the open latticework of the pencil-like *flèche,* or spire, on the roof—the design of the building is simplicity itself. In essence, it's no more than a thin, rectangular box, much taller than it is wide. The building is actually two chapels in one. The plainer, first-floor chapel was for servants and lowly members of the court. The infinitely more spectacular upper chapel, up a dark spiral staircase, was for the king and important members of the court. Here the glory of the chapel—the stained glass—is spectacularly intact. Notice how the walls, in fact, consist of at least twice as much glass as masonry: The entire aim of the architects was to provide the maximum amount of window space. Ste-Chapelle is one of the supreme achievements of the Middle Ages. Come early in the day to avoid the dutiful crowds that trudge around it. Better still, try to attend one of the regular, candle-lit concerts given here. ⊠ *In the Palais de Justice.* ☏ *01–43–54–30–09 for concert information.* 🎫 *32 frs.* ⊙ *Daily 9:30–6:30; winter, daily 10–6. Métro: Cité.*

⓱ **St-Louis-en-l'Ile.** The only church on the Ile St-Louis, built from 1664 to 1726 to the Baroque designs of Louis Le Vau, is lavishly furnished and has two unusual exterior features: its original pierced spire, holy in every sense, and an iron clock added in 1741. ⊠ *rue St-Louis-en-l'Ile. Métro: Pont-Marie.*

❻ **St-Séverin.** This unusually wide, Flamboyant Gothic church dominates a Left Bank neighborhood filled with squares and pedestrian streets. In the 11th century, the church that stood here was the parish church for the entire Left Bank. Louis XIV's cousin, a capricious woman known simply as the Grande Mademoiselle, adopted St-Séverin when she tired of St-Sulpice; she then spent vast sums getting court decorator Le Brun to modernize the chancel in the 16th century. Note the splendidly deviant spiraling column in the forest of pillars behind the altar. ✉ *rue des Prêtres St-Séverin.* ⊙ *Weekdays 11–5:30, Sat. 11–10. Métro: St-Michel.*

8 **La Sorbonne.** Named after Robert de Sorbon, a medieval canon who founded a theological college here in 1253 for 16 students, the Sorbonne is one of the oldest universities in Europe. For centuries it has been one of France's principal institutions of higher learning, as well as the hub of the Latin Quarter and nerve center of Paris's student population. The church and university buildings were restored by Cardinal Richelieu in the 17th century, and the maze of amphitheaters and lecture rooms retain a hallowed air. You can visit the main courtyard on rue de la Sorbonne and peek into the main lecture hall. The square is dominated by the university church, the noble **Église de la Sorbonne;** inside is the white marble tomb of that ultimate crafty cleric, Cardinal Richelieu himself. ✉ *rue de la Sorbonne. Métro: Cluny–La Sorbonne.*

FROM ORSAY TO ST-GERMAIN

This section covers the western half of the Left Bank, from the Musée d'Orsay in the stately 7ᵉ arrondissement, to the Faubourg St-Germain, a lively and colorful area in the 6ᵉ arrondissement. The Musée d'Orsay houses one of the world's most spectacular arrays of Impressionist paintings in a daringly converted Belle Epoque rail station on the Seine. Further along the river, the 18th-century Palais Bourbon, home to the National Assembly, sets the tone. Luxurious ministries and embassies line the surrounding streets, their majestic scale in total keeping with the Hôtel des Invalides, whose gold-leafed dome climbs heavenward above the regal tomb of Napoléon. The splendid Rodin Museum is only a short walk away.

To the east, the boulevard St-Michel slices the Left Bank in two: on one side, the Latin Quarter (☞ The Islands and the Latin Quarter, *above*); on the other, the Faubourg St-Germain, named for St-Germain-des-Prés, the oldest church in Paris. The venerable church tower has long acted as beacon for intellectuals, most famously during the 1950s when Albert Camus, Jean-Paul Sartre, and Simone de Beauvoir ate and drank existentialism in the neighborhood cafés such as Les Deux Magots and Café de Flore (☞ Chapter 3). A highlight of St-Germain is the Jardin du Luxembourg, the city's most famous and colorful park.

Numbers in the margin correspond to numbers on the Orsay to St-Germain map; these numbers indicate a suggested path for sightseeing.

Sights to See

❼ École Nationale des Beaux-Arts. The National Fine Arts College occupies three large mansions near the Seine. The school—today the breeding ground for painters, sculptors, and architects—was once the site of a convent. During the Revolution, the convent was used to safekeep artworks from impassioned mobs; if you wander into the courtyard and galleries of the school you can see casts and copies of these pieces. ⊠ *14 rue Bonaparte.* ☉ *Daily 1–7. Métro: St-Germain-des-Prés.*

❸ Hôtel des Invalides. Les Invalides, as it is widely known, is an outstanding monumental Baroque ensemble, designed by Libéral Bruand in the 1670s at the behest of Louis XIV to house wounded, or "invalid," soldiers. Although no more than a handful of old soldiers live at the Invalides today, the military link remains in the form of the **Musée de l'Armée,** one of the world's foremost military museums, with a vast, albeit musty, collection of arms, armor, uniforms, banners, and military pictures down through the ages.

★ The 17th-century **Église St-Louis des Invalides,** the Invalides's original church, was the site of the first performance of Berlioz's *Requiem,* in 1837. The most impressive dome in Paris towers over Jules Hardouin-Mansart's **Église du Dôme,** built onto the end of Église St-Louis but blocked off from it in 1793—no great pity, perhaps, as the two buildings are vastly different in style and scale. The remains of Napoléon are here, in a series of no fewer than six coffins, one inside the next, within a bombastic tomb of red porphyry. ⊠ *Esplanade des Invalides,* ☎ *01–44–42–37–67.* ▧ *35 frs.* ☉ *Daily 10–6; winter, daily 10–5.*

❾ Hôtel des Monnaies. Louis XVI transferred the Royal Mint to this imposing mansion in the late 18th century. Although the mint was moved again, to Pessac, near Bordeaux, in

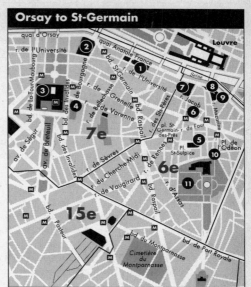

Orsay to St-Germain

1973, weights and measures, medals, and limited-edition coins are still made here. The **Musée de la Monnaie** (Coin Museum) has an extensive collection of coins, documents, engravings, and paintings. On Tuesday and Friday at 2 PM you can catch the coin metal craftsmen at work in their ateliers overlooking the Seine. ⌧ *11 quai de Conti.* 🎫 *20 frs, Sun. 15 frs.* ☉ *Tues., Thurs.–Sun. 1–6, Wed. 1–9. Métro: Pont-Neuf.*

❽ Institut de France. The Institute is one of France's most revered cultural institutions, and its curved, dome-topped facade is one of the Left Bank's most impressive waterside sights. It was built as a college in 1661; at the beginning of the 19th century, Napoléon stipulated that the Institute be transferred here from the Louvre. The Académie Française, the oldest of the five academies that compose the Institute, was created by Cardinal Richelieu in 1635. Its first major task was to edit the definitive French dictionary (which still isn't finished); it is also charged with safeguarding the purity of the French language. The appointment of historian and author Marguerite Yourcenar to the Académie in 1986 broke the centuries-old tradition of the academy as a male bastion. The Institute also embraces the Académie des Beaux-Arts, the Académie des Sciences, the Académie des Inscriptions et Belles Lettres, and the Académie des Sciences Morales et Politiques. ☒ *pl. de l'Institut. Guided visits reserved for cultural associations only. Métro: Pont-Neuf.*

🐾 ⓫ **Jardin du Luxembourg.** The Luxembourg Garden is one of the prettiest of Paris's few large parks. The fountains, ponds, trim hedges, precisely planted rows of trees, and gravel walks are typical of the French fondness for formal gardens. The 17th-century Palais du Luxembourg, which now houses the French Senate, provides an imposing backdrop. *Métro: Odéon; RER: Luxembourg.*

❶ **Musée d'Orsay.** Since opening in December 1986, the Musée d'Orsay—devoted to the arts (mainly French) spanning the period 1848–1914—has become one of the city's most popular museums. Once a train station, the marvelously transformed building still has its huge clocks; exhibits take up three floors, but the immediate impression is of a single, vast, stationlike hall. The chief artistic attraction is the Impressionists, whose works are displayed under the roof. Renoir, Sisley, Pissarro, and Monet are all well represented. Highlights include Monet's *Poppy Field* and Renoir's *Le Moulin de la Galette,* which differs from many other Impressionist paintings in that Renoir worked from numerous studies and completed it in his studio rather than painting it in the open air. The post-Impressionists—Cézanne, van Gogh, Gauguin, and Toulouse-Lautrec—are also represented on the top floor.

On the first floor, you'll find the work of Manet and the delicate nuances of Degas. Be sure to see Manet's *Déjeuner sur l'Herbe,* the painting that scandalized Paris in 1863 at the Salon des Refusés, an exhibit organized by artists refused permission to show their work at the Academy's official annual salon.

Thought-provoking sculptures litter the museum at every turn. Two further highlights are the faithfully restored Belle Epoque restaurant and the model of the entire Opéra quarter, displayed beneath a glass floor. ☒ *1 rue de Bellechasse,* ☎ *01–40–49–48–84.* 🎫 *36 frs, Sun. 24 frs.* ☉ *Tues.–Sat.*

10–6, Thurs. 10–9:30, Sun. 9–6. Métro: Solférino; RER: Musée d'Orsay.

④ Musée Rodin. The splendid Hôtel Biron retains much of its 18th-century atmosphere and makes a gracious setting for the sculpture of Auguste Rodin (1840–1917). You'll doubtless recognize the seated *Thinker,* with his elbow resting on his knee, and the passionate *Kiss.* Don't go without visiting the garden: It is exceptional both for its rosebushes (more than 2,000 of them, representing 100 varieties) and for its sculpture, including a powerful statue of the novelist Balzac and the despairing group of medieval city fathers known as the *Burghers of Calais.* ✉ *77 rue de Varenne,* ☎ *01–44–18–61–10.* ▭ *28 frs, Sun. 18 frs.* ☉ *Easter–Oct., Tues.–Sun. 10–6; Nov.–Easter, Tues.–Sun. 10–5. Métro: Varenne.*

② Palais Bourbon. The most prominent feature of the home of the Assemblée Nationale (French Parliament) is its colonnaded facade, commissioned by Napoléon. It was cleaned at the start of the decade (although jeopardized at one stage by political squabbles as to whether cleaning should begin from the left or the right) and is now a sparkling sight. ✉ *pl. du Palais-Bourbon.* ☉ *During temporary exhibits only. Métro: Assemblée Nationale.*

⑥ St-Germain-des-Prés. Paris's oldest church was first built to shelter a relic of the true cross, brought back from Spain in AD 542. The chancel was enlarged and the church then consecrated by Pope Alexander III in 1163; the tall, sturdy tower—a Left Bank landmark—dates from this period. The church stages superb organ concerts and recitals. ✉ *pl. St-Germain-des-Prés.* ☉ *Weekdays 8–7:30; weekends 8–9. Métro: St-Germain-des-Prés.*

⑤ St-Sulpice. Dubbed the Cathedral of the Left Bank, this enormous 17th-century church has entertained some unlikely christenings—the Marquis de Sade's and Charles Baudelaire's, for instance—and the nuptials of irreverent wordsmith Victor Hugo. The 18th-century facade was never finished, and its unequal towers add a playful touch to an otherwise sober design. The interior is baldly impersonal, despite the magnificent Delacroix frescoes—notably *Jacob*

Wrestling with the Angel—in the first chapel on your right. ✉ *pl. St-Sulpice. Métro: St-Sulpice.*

⑩ Théâtre de l'Odéon. At the north end of the Luxembourg Gardens, on place de l'Odéon, sits the colonnaded Odéon theater. It is currently the French home of the Theater of Europe and stages excellent productions by major foreign companies, sometimes in English (☞ Chapter 5). ✉ *pl. de l'Odéon,* ☎ *01–44–41–36–36. Métro: Odéon.*

MONTPARNASSE

A mile to the south of the Seine lies the district of Montparnasse, named after Mount Parnassus, the Greek mountain associated with the worship of Apollo and the Muses. Montparnasse's cultural heyday came in the first four decades of the 20th century, when it replaced Montmartre as *the* place for painters and poets to live. Pablo Picasso, Amedeo Modigliani, Ernest Hemingway, Jean Cocteau, and Trotsky were among the luminaries who spawned an intellectual café society—later to be found at St-Germain (☞ From Orsay to St-Germain, *above*)—and prompted the launch of a string of arty brasseries along the district's main thoroughfare, the broad boulevard du Montparnasse.

The boulevard may lack poetic charm these days, but nightlife stays the pace as bars, clubs, restaurants, and cinemas crackle with energy beneath continental Europe's tallest high-rise: the 59-story Tour Montparnasse. While the Tower itself is a typically bland product of the early 1970s, several more adventurous buildings have risen in its wake. If you have a deeper feel for history, you may prefer the sumptuous Baroque church of Val-de-Grâce or the quiet earth of Montparnasse cemetery, where Baudelaire, Sartre, and Bartholdi (who designed the *Statue of Liberty*) slumber. The Paris underground had its headquarters nearby—in the Roman catacombs—during the Nazi occupation. After ignoring Hitler's orders to blow up the city, it was in Montparnasse that Governor von Choltitz signed the German surrender in August 1944.

Numbers in the margin correspond to numbers on the Montparnasse map; these numbers indicate a suggested path for sightseeing.

Sights to See

4 **Catacombs.** Enter the Paris catacombs, originally built by the Romans to quarry stone, from aptly named place Denfert-Rochereau: *denfert* is a corruption of the French for hell, *enfer*. The catacombs, which tunnel under much of the Left Bank, were used to store millions of skeletons from disused graveyards; during World War II, they were the headquarters of the French Resistance. Take a flashlight. ⊠ *1 pl. Denfert-Rochereau,* ☎ *01–43–22–47–63.* 💳 *27 frs.* ⊙ *Tues.–Fri. 2–4, weekends 9–11 and 2–4. Guided tours on Wed. at 2:45; 20 frs extra. Métro and RER: Denfert-Rochereau.*

3 **Cimetière de Montparnasse.** This cemetery is not terribly picturesque but it contains many of the quarter's most illustrious residents, buried only a stone's throw away from where they lived and loved: Charles Baudelaire, Auguste Bartholdi (who designed the Statue of Liberty), Alfred Dreyfus, Guy de Maupassant, Jean-Paul Sartre, and, more recently, photographer Man Ray, playwright Samuel Beckett, actress Jean Seberg, and singer-songwriter Serge Gainsbourg. ⊠ *Entrances: rue Froidevaux, bd. Edgar-Quinet. Métro: Raspail, Gaîté.*

6 **Closerie des Lilas.** Now a pricey bar-restaurant, the Closerie remains a staple of all literary tours of Paris. Commemorative plaques fastened to the bar mark the places where litterati like Baudelaire, Verlaine, Hemingway, and Apollinaire used to station themselves. ⊠ *171 bd. du Montparnasse,* ☎ *01–43–26–70–50. Métro: Vavin; RER: Port-Royal.*

5 **Fondation Cartier.** Architect Jean Nouvel's eye-catching giant glass cubicle is a suitable setting for the temporary, thought-provoking shows of contemporary art organized here by jewelry giant Cartier. ⊠ *261 bd. Raspail,* ☎ *01–42–18–56–50.* 💳 *30 frs.* ⊙ *Tues.–Sun. noon–8. Métro: Raspail.*

1 **Place du 18-Juin-1940.** This square beneath the Tour Montparnasse is significant in World War II history. It is named

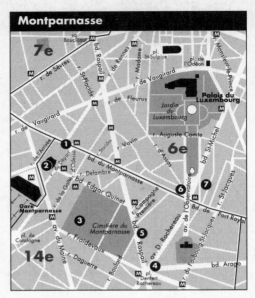

for the date of the radio speech Charles de Gaulle broadcast from London, urging the French to resist the Germans after the Nazi invasion of May 1940. And it was here that German military governor Dietrich von Choltitz surrendered to the Allies in August 1944, ignoring Hitler's orders to destroy the city as he withdrew. A plaque on the wall of what is now a shopping center—originally the Montparnasse train station extended this far—commemorates the event. *Métro: Montparnasse-Bienvenue.*

② **Tour Montparnasse.** As continental Europe's tallest skyscraper, completed in 1973, this 685-foot tower offers a stupendous view of Paris from its open-air roof terrace. If you go to the top-floor bar for drinks, the ride up is free. Banal by day, the tower becomes Montparnasse's neon-lit beacon at night. ⊠ *33 av. du Maine.* ☎ *42 frs.* ⊘ *Apr.–Sept., daily 9:30 AM–11:30 PM; Oct.–Mar., Sun.–Thurs. 9:30 AM–10:30 PM, Fri.–Sat. 9:30 AM–11 PM. Métro: Montparnasse-Bienvenue.*

⑦ **Val de Grâce.** This imposing 17th-century Left Bank church, extensively restored in the early 1990s, has a powerfully rhythmic two-story facade that rivals the Dôme Church at the Invalides as the city's most striking example of Italianate Baroque. Pierre Mignard's 1663 cupola fresco features more than 200 sky-climbing figures. ⊠ *1 pl. Alphonse-Laveran. RER: Port-Royal.*

MONTMARTRE

On a dramatic rise above the city is Montmartre, site of the Sacré-Coeur basilica and home to a once-thriving artistic community, which included Henri de Toulouse-Lautrec, Pablo Picasso, and Salvador Dali. Although the fabled nightlife of old Montmartre has fizzled down to some glitzy nightclubs and porn shows, Montmartre still exudes a sense of history, a timeless quality infused with that hard-to-define Gallic charm.

Visiting Montmartre means negotiating a lot of steep streets and flights of steps. The crown atop this urban peak, Sacré-Coeur, is something of an architectural oddity. It has been called everything from grotesque to sublime; its silhouette, viewed from afar at dusk or sunrise, looks more like a mosque than a cathedral.

Numbers in the margin correspond to numbers on the Montmartre map; these numbers indicate a suggested path for sightseeing.

Sights to See

❻ Bateau-Lavoir. Montmartre poet Max Jacob coined the name, meaning Boat Wash House, for the original building on this site, which burned down in 1970. He said it resembled a boat and that the warren of artists' studios within was perpetually paint-splattered and in need of a good hosing down. It was in the original Bateau-Lavoir that, early this century, Pablo Picasso and Georges Braque made their first bold stabs at the concept of Cubism—a move that paved the way for abstract painting. The poet Guillaume Apollinaire also had a studio here; his book *Les Peintures du Cubisme* (1913) set the seal on the movement's historical acceptance. The new building also contains art studios, but, if you didn't know its history, you'd probably walk right past it; it is the epitome of poured concrete drabness. ✉ *13 pl. Emile-Goudeau. Métro: Abbesses.*

⑧ Espace Dali. Some of Salvador Dali's less familiar works are among the 25 sculptures and 300 prints housed in this museum. The atmosphere is meant to approximate the surreal experience, with black walls, low lighting, and a New Agey musical score—punctuated by recordings of Dali's own voice. ✉ *11 rue Poulbot,* ☎ *01–42–64–40–10.* 🎫 *35 frs.* ☉ *Daily 10–6; summer, daily 10–8. Métro: Abbesses.*

⑪ Lapin Agile. This bar-cabaret was originally one of the raunchiest haunts in Montmartre. It got its curious name—the Nimble Rabbit—when the owner, André Gill, hung up a sign (now in the Musée du Vieux Montmartre) of a laughing rabbit jumping out of a saucepan clutching a bottle of wine. In 1903, the premises were bought by the most celebrated cabaret entrepreneur of them all, Aristide Bruand, portrayed by Toulouse-Lautrec in a series of famous posters. Today, it manages to preserve at least something of its earlier flavor, unlike the Moulin Rouge. ✉ *22 rue des Saules,* ☎ *01–46–06–85–87. Métro: Lamarck-Caulaincourt.*

② Moulin de la Galette. This windmill, on a hillock shrouded by shrubbery, is one of two remaining windmills in Montmartre. It was once the focal point of an open-air cabaret made famous in a painting by Renoir. Unfortunately, it is now privately owned and can only be admired from the street below. ✉ *rue Tholozé. Métro: Abbesses.*

① Moulin Rouge. This world-famous cabaret was built in 1885 as a windmill, then transformed into a dance hall in 1900. Those wild, early days were immortalized by Toulouse-Lautrec in his posters and paintings. It still trades shamelessly on the notion of Paris as a city of sin (☞ Chapter 5). The cancan, by the way—still a regular feature here—was considerably more raunchy when Toulouse-Lautrec was around. ✉ *82 bd. de Clichy,* ☎ *01–46–06–00–19. Métro: Blanche.*

⑩ Musée du Vieux Montmartre. In its turn-of-the-century heyday, Montmartre's historical museum was home to an illustrious group of painters, writers, and assorted cabaret artists. Foremost among them were Renoir—he painted the

Montmartre

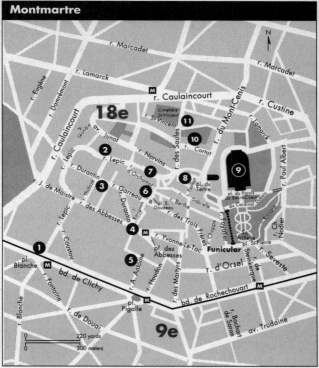

Bateau-Lavoir, **6**

Espace Dali, **8**

Lapin Agile, **11**

Moulin de la Galette, **2**

Moulin Rouge, **1**

Musée du Vieux Montmartre, **10**

Place des Abbesses, **4**

Place Jean-Baptiste Clément, **7**

Sacré-Coeur, **9**

Studio 28, **3**

Théâtre Libre, **5**

Moulin de la Galette, an archetypal Parisian scene of sun-drenched revelers, while he lived here—and Maurice Utrillo, Montmartre painter par excellence. Utrillo evoked the atmosphere of old Montmartre hauntingly: To help convey the decaying buildings of the area, he mixed plaster and sand with his paints. The museum also provides a view of the tiny **vineyard**—the only one in Paris—on neighboring rue des Saules. A symbolic 125 gallons of wine are still produced every year. It's hardly vintage stuff, but there are predictably bacchanalian celebrations during the harvest on the first weekend of October. ⊠ *12 rue Cortot,* ☏ *01–46–06–61–11.* ☞ *25 frs.* ☉ *Tues.–Sun. 11–6. Métro: Lamarck-Caulaincourt.*

❹ Place des Abbesses. This triangular square is typical of the picturesque, slightly countrified style that has made Montmartre famous. The entrance to the Abbesses métro station, a curving, sensuous mass of iron, is one of the two original Art Nouveau entrance canopies left in Paris. *Métro: Abbesses.*

❼ Place Jean-Baptiste Clément. Painter Amedeo Modigliani (1884–1920) had a studio here at No. 7. Some say he was the greatest Italian artist of the 20th century, fusing the genius of the Renaissance with the modernity of Cézanne and Picasso. He claimed that he would drink himself to death—he eventually did—and chose the right part of town to do it in. ⊠ *pl. Jean-Baptiste Clément. Métro: Abbesses.*

❾ Sacré-Coeur. The white domes of the Sacred Heart Basilica patrol the Paris skyline from the top of Montmartre. The French government decided to erect Sacré-Coeur in 1873, as a sort of national guilt offering in expiation for the blood shed during the Commune and Franco-Prussian War in 1870–71. Building lasted until World War I; the basilica was not consecrated until 1919. Stylistically, the Sacré-Coeur borrows elements from Romanesque and Byzantine models. This cavernous building with a scaly, pointed dome is strangely disjointed and unsettling. The gloomy interior is worth visiting for its golden mosaics. ⊠ *pl. du Parvis-du-Sacré-Coeur. Métro: Anvers.*

❸ Studio 28. What looks like no more than a generic little movie theater has a distinguished dramatic history: When it opened in 1928, it was the first purposely built for *art et essai,* or experimental theater, in the world. Over the years, the movies of directors like Jean Cocteau, François Truffaut, and Orson Welles have been shown here before their official premieres. ✉ *10 rue Tholozé,* ☎ *01–46–06–36–07. Métro: Abbesses.*

⑤ Théâtre Libre. The Free Theater was founded in 1887 by André Antoine and was immensely influential in popularizing the work of iconoclastic young playwrights such as Ibsen and Strindberg. ✉ *37 rue André-Antoine. Métro: Abbesses.*

3 Dining

Updated
by
Alexander
Lobrano

PARIS REMAINS THE ULTIMATE gourmet destination. Nonetheless, if you are coming from New York, London, or Los Angeles, where innovative restaurants abound, you may find the French capital a little staid. In fact, there is a currently a battle waging between the traditionalists and a remarkable new generation of chefs who are modernizing French cuisine. The upshot is lighter fare with vegetables and fish alongside the French classics.

Parisians now insist that you can dine just as well at one of the new breed of bistro run by young, upstart chefs as you can at a fancier, more established, more expensive place. The new bistros are very popular, so make reservations as soon as you arrive. Because many places serve a market menu, meaning that the chef shops daily and buys according to what's in season or well-priced, many of the dishes mentioned in our reviews are cited more to give you an idea of a restaurant's cooking style than as specific recommendations.

Facing a penny-wise public, many Paris restaurateurs now offer prix-fixe (fixed-price) dining and bistro fare at the best prices in years. Still, it's not unusual to hear tales of outrageous prices, mediocre food, and haughty service. It's certainly possible to have a bad meal here. Yet the city's restaurants exist principally for the demanding Parisians themselves, for whom every meal is, if not a way of life, certainly an event worthy of their undivided attention. To dine well, therefore, look for restaurants where the French go—even if they are off the beaten path. Keep in mind, however, that world-famous restaurants are bound to be frequented by foreigners as well as Parisians and that an American at the next table is not always a bad sign.

Included in this listing are a variety of restaurants and price ranges, from formal dining rooms serving haute cuisine to cheery bistros offering hearty French cooking. More than half are in the 1er–8e arrondissements, within easy reach of hotels and sights. Recognizing that even in Paris many people might not want to eat French food at every meal, several ethnic restaurants are listed.

A **restaurant** traditionally serves a three-course meal (first, main, and dessert) at both lunch and dinner. Although this category includes the most formal, three-star establishments, it also applies to humble neighborhood spots. Don't expect to grab a quick snack. In general, restaurants are what you choose when you want a complete meal and when you have the time to linger over it. Hours are fairly consistent (☞ *below*).

Many say that **bistros** served the world's first fast food. After the fall of Napoléon, the Russian soldiers who occupied Paris were known to bang on zinc-topped café bars, crying "bistro"—"hurry" in Russian. Although many nowadays are quite upscale, most remain cozy establishments serving straightforward, frequently gutsy cooking, a wide variety of meats, and long-simmered dishes such as pot-au-feu. **Brasseries**—ideal places for quick, one-dish meals, often with *choucroute* (sauerkraut and sausages) on the menu—typically keep late hours. Some are open 24 hours a day—a good thing to know, since many restaurants stop serving at 10:30 PM.

Like bistros and brasseries, **cafés** come in a confusing variety. Usually informal neighborhood hangouts, cafés may also be veritable showplaces attracting chic, well-heeled crowds. At most cafés, regulars congregate at the bar, where coffee and drinks are cheaper than at tables. At lunch, tables are set and a limited menu is served. Sandwiches are served throughout the day. Cafés are for lingering, for people-watching, and for daydreaming; they are listed separately below.

Wine bars, or bistros *à vins,* are a newer phenomenon. These informal places serve very limited menus, often no more than open-face sandwiches (*tartines*) and selections of cheeses and cold cuts (*charcuterie*). Some wine bars are very fancy indeed, with costly wine lists and full menus, but most remain friendly and unassuming places for sampling wines you might otherwise never try (☞ Chapter 5, for a more comprehensive list of wine bars).

Generally, Paris restaurants are open from noon to about 2 and from 7:30 or 8 to 10 or 10:30. Assume a restaurant is open every day unless otherwise indicated. Surprisingly, many prestigious restaurants close on Saturday as well as Sunday. July and August are the most common months for annual closings, but Paris in August is no longer the wasteland it used to be.

In the reviews below, we have only indicated where reservations are essential (and when booking weeks or months in advance is necessary) and where reservations are not accepted. Because restaurants are open for only a few hours for lunch and dinner, and because meals are long affairs here, we urge you to make reservations. Most wine bars do not take reservations; reservations are also unnecessary for brasserie and café meals at odd hours. If you want to sit in a no-smoking section, make this clear; the mandatory no-smoking area is sometimes limited to a very few tables and often not strictly enforced.

All establishments must post their menus outside, so study them carefully before deciding to enter. Most restaurants offer two basic types of menu: à la carte and fixed price (prix fixe, or *un menu*). The prix-fixe menu will usually offer the best value, though choices are limited. Most menus begin with a first course (*une entrée*), often subdivided into cold and hot starters, followed by fish and poultry, then meat; it's rare today that anyone orders something from all three. However, outside of brasseries, wine bars, and other simple places, it's inappropriate to order just one dish, as you'll understand when you see the waiter's expression. In recent years, the *menu dégustation* has become popular; consisting of numerous small courses, it allows for a wide sampling of the chef's offerings.

Perhaps surprisingly, casual dress is acceptable at all but the fanciest restaurants. Be aware that in Paris, casual does not mean without style. When in doubt, leave the blue jeans behind, and unless you want to be instantly identified as a tourist, don't wear sneakers. Use your judgment. In the reviews below, we have indicated where a jacket and/or tie are required.

Prices

Although prices are high, we have made an effort to include a number of lower-priced establishments. Prices include tax and tip (*service compris* or *prix nets*), but pocket change left on the table in basic places, or an additional 5% in better restaurants, is appreciated.

CATEGORY	COST*
$$$$	over 550 frs.
$$$	300 frs.–550 frs.
$$	175 frs.–300 frs.
$	under 175 frs.

per person for a three-course meal, including tax and service but not drinks

Restaurants

1er Arrondissement (Louvre/Les Halles)

$$$$ ✕ **Le Grand Véfour.** Luminaries from Napoléon to Colette to Jean Cocteau frequented this intimate address under the arcades of the Palais-Royal; you can request to be seated at their preferred tables. A sumptuously decorated restaurant, its 18th-century origins make it one of the oldest in Paris. Chef Guy Martin impresses with his unique blend of sophisticated yet rustic dishes, including roast lamb in a jus of herbs. ⊠ *17 rue Beaujolais,* ☎ *01–42–96–56–27. Reservations essential 1 wk in advance. Jacket and tie. AE, DC, MC, V. Closed weekends and Aug. Métro: Palais-Royal.*

$$–$$$ ✕ **Chez Pauline.** In this venerable bistro, the doorman in livery sets the tone—service is solicitous and unfailingly correct. Indulge in classic luxury foods like foie gras, truffles, and fine seafood. Fans of crème brûlée take note of Chez Pauline's version: four different individual portions in little china ramekins. ⊠ *5 rue Villedo,* ☎ *01–42–96–20--70. Reservations essential. AE, DC, MC, V. Closed Sun. No lunch Sat. Métro: Pyramides.*

$$ ✕ **Il Ristorantino.** Chef Ciro Polge serves some of the best Italian food in Paris at this small place done in minimalist Milanese style. The fettucine with a ragu of shellfish in a rich tomato sauce and the *fritto misto* (vegetables dipped in a delicate batter and fried) are particularly good. The wine list is excellent, if short on affordable bottles. ⊠ *6 rue d'Argenteuil,* ☎ *01–42–60–56–22. AE, DC, MC, V. Closed Sun. No lunch Sat. Métro: Louvre.*

$–$$ ✕ **Aux Crus de Bourgogne.** The din of a happy crowd fills this delightful, old-fashioned bistro with bright lights and red-checker tablecloths. It opened in 1932 and quickly became popular by serving two luxury items— foie gras and cold lobster with homemade mayonnaise— at surprisingly low prices, a tradition that happily continues. ⊠ *3 rue Bachaumont,* ☎ *01–42–33–48–24. V. Closed weekends and Aug. Métro: Sentier.*

$ ✕ **Café Marly.** The latest venture of the Costes brothers is one of the chicest places in Paris for a drink or a light meal—perhaps an omelet or a salad. The splendid view of the Louvre Pyramid and—depending on where you're sitting—the Eiffel Tower makes this one of the best fresh-air venues in Paris. Inside, the ebonized moldings and crimson walls create a dramatic mood at night. ⊠ *Musée du Louvre, Cour Napoléon, 93 rue de Rivoli,* ☎ *01–49–26–06–60. MC, V. Reservations not accepted. Métro: Palais-Royal.*

$ ✕ **Le Moi.** At this superb Vietnamese restaurant, you can sample *nems* (deep-fried mini spring rolls) or steamed dumplings. The poultry, beef, or seafood salads are enlivened with fresh Asian herbs like lemongrass and lemon basil. Service is prompt and friendly. ⊠ *5 rue Danou,* ☎ *01–47–03–92–05. MC, V. Closed Sun. No lunch Sat. Métro: Opéra.*

2e Arrondissement (Le Bourse)

$$ ✕ **Chez Georges.** The food isn't bad, but the atmosphere is better. A wood-paneled entry leads you to an elegant and unpretentious dining room. One long, white-clothed stretch of tables lines the mirrored walls, and attentive waiters sweep efficiently along the entire length. Enjoy the herring, sole, and a phenomenally tender steak. ⊠ *1 rue du Mail,* ☎ *01–42–60–07–11. AE, DC, MC, V. Closed Sun. and Aug. Métro: Sentier.*

$–$$ ✕ **Le Brin de Zinc et Madame.** A bustling old-fashioned
★ place, this spot is ideal for an easygoing night on the town. The decor and the service are a bit rough-and-tumble, but the food is delicious and generously portioned. Main dishes, such as grilled salmon or roast chicken, are served with sautéed potatoes and vegetables; the excellent tarts are homemade. ⊠ *50 rue Montorgueil,* ☎

01–42–21–10–80. AE, MC, V. No lunch Sun. Métro: Etienne-Marcel.

3ᵉ Arrondissement (Beaubourg/Marais)

$$ ✕ **Chez Janou.** With its pretty art-nouveau tiles and potted plants, this tiny place is the very definition of a neighborhood bistro. Check the daily specials—in season, try the sautéed wild mushrooms—or homey classics, like confit de canard or hearty braised veal shank. ✉ *2 rue Roger-Verlomme,* ☎ *01–42–72–28–41. MC, V. Closed weekends. Métro: Bastille.*

$ ✕ **Chez Jenny.** Since the installation of a rotisserie grill, this place is home to what is probably the most delicious choucroute *garnie* (with sausage) in the capital. The sauerkraut, delivered weekly by a private supplier in Alsace, is garnished with a variety of Alsatian charcuterie and a big grilled ham knuckle. ✉ *39 bd. du Temple,* ☎ *01–42–74–75–75. AE, DC, MC, V. Métro: République.*

$ ✕ **Chez Omar.** Whether you're a die-hard couscous fan or have never tried it before, this is the place for this signature North African dish. Order it with grilled skewered lamb, spicy *merguez* sausage, a lamb shank, or chicken—portions are generous. Proprietor Omar Guerida is famously friendly and speaks English. ✉ *47 rue de Bretagne,* ☎ *01–42–72–36–26. MC, V. No lunch Sun. Métro: Filles du Calvaire.*

4ᵉ Arrondissement (Marais/Ile St-Louis)

$$$$ ✕ **L'Ambroisie.** This tiny, romantic restaurant on the patrician place des Vosges is one of the best in Paris. Chef-owner Bernard Pacaud's refined, oft-imitated cuisine, including such dishes as mousse of red bell peppers and braised oxtail, is served in a jewel-like Italianate setting of flowers, tapestries, and subdued lighting. ✉ *9 pl. des Vosges,* ☎ *01–42–78–51–45. Reservations 1 month in advance essential. MC, V. Closed Sun., Mon., Aug., and mid-Feb. Métro: St-Paul.*

$$ ✕ **Au Bourguignon du Marais.** The handsome, con-
★ temporary decor of this Marais bistro and wine bar offers a perfect backdrop for the good, traditional fare (steak tartare, escargots) and excellent Burgundies served by the glass and bottle. ✉ *19 rue de Jouy,* ☎ *01–48–87–15–40. MC, V. Closed Sun. Métro: St-Paul.*

$$ ✕ **Le Maraîcher.** With its exposed stone walls and wood beams, this intimate restaurant on a quiet street in the Marais is very *vieux Paris*. The owner worked at the renowned Lucas-Carton, which may account for the table settings and service, which are surprisingly refined considering the reasonable prices. Roasted lamb fillet with eggplant and coquilles St-Jacques with potato pulp in a balsamic vinaigrette are good choices. ⊠ *5 rue Beautreillis,* ☎ *01–42–71–42–49. MC, V. Closed Sun., late July–early Aug. No lunch Sat. Métro: Sully-Morland.*

$$ ✕ **Le Vieux Bistro.** Overlook the touristy location next to Notre-Dame and the corny name, "the old bistro." This place really *is* generations old, and its menu is full of bistro classics, such as beef fillet with marrow, éclairs, and tart Tatin. ⊠ *14 rue du Cloître-Notre-Dame,* ☎ *01–43–54–18–95. MC, V. Métro: Hôtel de Ville.*

$–$$ ✕ **Bofinger.** One of the oldest, most beautiful, and most popular brasseries in Paris has been much improved since brasserie maestro Jean-Paul Bucher took over. Settle in under the gorgeous art-nouveau glass cupola, and enjoy fine classic brasserie fare, such as oysters, grilled sole, or fillet of lamb. Note that the no-smoking section here is not only enforced, but is also in the prettiest part of the restaurant. ⊠ *5–7 rue de la Bastille,* ☎ *01–42–72–87–82. AE, DC, MC, V. Métro: Bastille.*

$ ✕ **Baracane.** The owner of this small, simple place oversees the menu of robust specialties of his native southwest France, including rabbit confit, veal tongue, and pear poached in wine and cassis. A reasonable dinner menu and cheaper menu at lunch keep the Baracane solidly affordable and one of the best values in the Marais. Service is friendly. ⊠ *38 rue des Tournelles,* ☎ *01–42–71–43–33. MC, V. Closed Sun. No lunch Sat. Métro: Bastille.*

$ ✕ **La Truffe.** In this attractive open-space restaurant with a mezzanine, you can find organic, vegetarian food that is prepared without fat or steaming—they use special cooking equipment so that the grains, mushrooms, and vegetables conserve their taste. Smoking is not allowed. ⊠ *31 rue Vieille-du-Temple,* ☎ *01–42–71–08–39. MC, V. Métro: St-Paul.*

5e Arrondissement (Latin Quarter)

$$$$ ✗ **La Tour d'Argent.** Dining at this temple to haute cuisine is an event—from apéritifs in the ground-floor bar to dinner in the top-floor dining room, with its breathtaking view of Notre-Dame. The food, unfortunately, does not reach the same heights as the setting. La Tour classics such as *caneton Tour d'Argent* (pressed duck) and *filets de sole Cardinal* have been lightened and contemporary creations added, including scallop salad with truffles. The wine list is one of the greatest in the world—visit the cellars before or after your meal. The lunch menu is relatively affordable. ⊠ *15 quai de la Tournelle,* ☎ *01–43–54–23–31. Reservations essential at least 1 wk in advance. Jacket and tie at dinner. AE, DC, MC, V. Closed Mon. Métro: Cardinal Lemoine.*

$ ✗ **Chantairelle.** The owners of this friendly restaurant
★   want to give you the full Auvergne experience, hence the decor: recycled barn timbers and a little stone fountain, along with a selection of essential oils diffusing local scents. This is hearty, rustic food, so only order an appetizer if you're really hungry. The copious main courses include stuffed cabbage and *potée,* a casserole of pork and vegetables in broth. ⊠ *17 rue Laplace,* ☎ *01–46– 33–18–59. MC, V. Closed Sun. No lunch Sat. Métro: Maubert-Mutualité.*

$ ✗ **Chez Toutoune.** This spacious restaurant with a cheery Provençal theme is owned and run by Colette Toutoune, one of the most respected female chefs in Paris. All meals begin with complimentary soup—usually vegetable. The main course may be roasted salmon with tomato confit or veal kidneys with bacon and spinach. Consider splurging on a bottle of velvety, red Domaine de la Bernarde 1991 from the admirable wine list. ⊠ *5 rue de Pontoise,* ☎ *01–43–26–56–81. AE, MC, V. Closed Sun., Mon., and Aug. Métro: Maubert-Mutualité.*

6e Arrondissement (St-Germain-des-Prés)

$$ ✗ **La Bastide Odéon.** This little corner of Provence in
★   Paris is just a few steps from the Luxembourg Gardens. Chef Gilles Ajuelos cooks wonderful pastas, such as tagliatelle in *pistou* (basil and pine nuts) with wild mush-

rooms, and delightful main courses, like peppered tuna steak with ratatouille. ⊠ *7 rue Corneille,* ☎ *01–43–26–03–65. MC, V. Closed weekends. Métro: Odéon; RER: Luxembourg.*

$$ ✕ **Les Bookinistes.** Talented chef Guy Savoy's fifth bistro is a big success with locals. The cheery post-modern dining room, painted peach, with red, blue, and yellow wall sconces, looks out on the Seine. The French country menu changes seasonally and might include a mussel and pumpkin soup or baby chicken roasted in a casserole with root vegetables. ⊠ *53 quai des Grands-Augustins,* ☎ *01–43–25–45–94. AE, DC, MC, V. Closed Sun. No lunch Sat. Métro: St-Michel.*

$–$$ ✕ **Le Bouillon Racine.** Originally a *bouillon,* a Parisian soup restaurant popular at the turn of the century, this two-story place is now a delightfully renovated Belle Epoque oasis with a good Belgian menu. The *waterzooie* (stewed chicken and vegetables) is an excellent main dish; for dessert try the odd-sounding but delicious moka-beer mousse with malt sauce. In honor of Belgium's some 400 different brews, there's a wonderful selection of beers. ⊠ *3 rue Racine,* ☎ *01–44–32–15–60. Reservations essential. AE, MC, V. Closed Sun. Métro: Odéon.*

7e Arrondissement (Invalides)

$$$$ ✕ **Jules Verne.** Distinctive all-black decor, stylish service, and top-ranked chef Alain Reix's cuisine—not to mention a location at 400 feet, on the second level of the Eiffel Tower—make the Jules Verne one of the hardest dinner reservations to get in Paris. Soufflé of giant crab and lobster tournedos in a veal and butter sauce are examples of Reix's colorful, flavorful dishes. Come for lunch—a table is easier to snag. ⊠ *Eiffel Tower,* ☎ *01–45–55–61–44. Reservations essential (reserve 2 months in advance for dinner at window table). Jacket and tie. AE, DC, MC, V. Métro: Bir-Hakeim.*

$$$–$$$$ ✕ **Paul Minchelli.** Don't come to this very sleek restaurant expecting elaborate sauces—Minchelli is a minimalist who believes that seasonings should not distract from the taste of his impeccably fresh catch-of-the-day. The baby clams with garlic and fiery espelette peppers as well as the sea bass drizzled with lemon and olive oil are just

Paris Dining

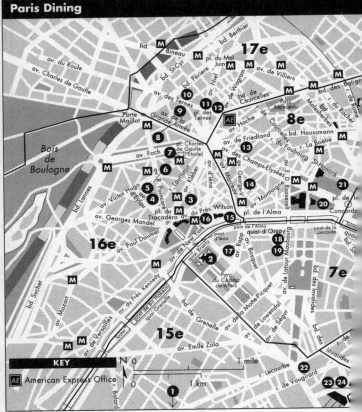

KEY

AE American Express Office

N 0 ——— 1 mile
0 ——— 1 km

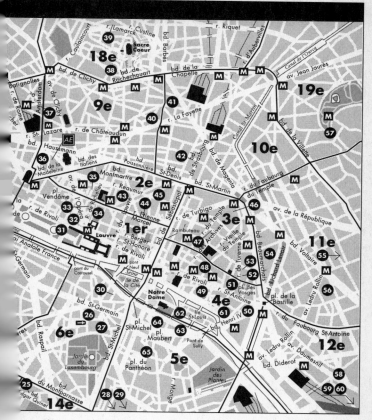

Chez Toutoune, **64**	Il Ristoratino, **32**	Paul Minchelli, **19**	Thoumieux, **18**
La Coupole, **25**	Jacques Mélac, **55**	Le Petit Rétro, **5**	Le Timgad, **8**
La Dinée, **1**	Jamin, **16**	Philippe Detourbe, **22**	La Tour d'Argent, **63**
La Ferme St-Hubert, **36**	Jules Verne, **2**	Pierre Gagnaire, **15**	La Truffe, **48**
La Fermette Marbeuf, **14**	Ledoyen, **20**	Prunier, **7**	La Verriere, **57**
Le Grand Véfour, **34**	Le Maraîcher, **61**	La Régalade, **24**	Le Vieux Bistro, **62**
Guy Savoy, **11**	Le Moi, **35**	Le Relais du Parc, **4**	Les Zygomates, **58**
L'Huitrier, **12**	Montparnasse 25, **23**	Le Restaurant, **38**	
	L'Oulette, **60**	Taillevent, **13**	

a few of his wonderful dishes. ✉ *54 bd. de La Tour-Maubourg,* ☎ *01–47–05–89–86. MC, V. Closed Sun., Mon. Métro: École Militaire.*

$–$$ ✕ **Au Bon Accueil.** If you want to see what well-heeled
★ Parisians like to eat these days, book a table at this extremely popular bistro as soon as you get to town. The excellent, reasonably priced *cuisine du marché* (daily menu based on what's in the markets) has made it a hit. Desserts are homemade and delicious, from the fruit tarts to the superb *pistache,* a pastry curl filled with homemade pistachio ice cream. ✉ *14 rue de Montessuy,* ☎ *01–47–05–46–11. Reservations essential. MC, V. Closed Sun. Métro, RER: Pont l'Alma.*

$ ✕ **Thoumieux.** Foie gras, rillettes, duck confit, cassoulet, and superb desserts are all made on the premises at this third-generation restaurant. The red velour banquettes, yellow walls, and bustling waiters in long, white aprons are delightfully Parisian. ✉ *79 rue St-Dominique,* ☎ *01–47–05–49–75. MC, V. Métro: Invalides.*

8ᵉ Arrondissement (Champs-Elysées)

$$$$ ✕ **Les Ambassadeurs.** This restaurant in the opulent Crillon hotel is undoubtedly the finest in Paris. Respected chef Christian Constant is a master at giving even the humblest ingredients sophistication, as exemplified by his petit salé of cod, rabbit with marjoram, and pork with spider crab. Some find the all-marble dining room a bit inhospitable, but no one can fault the view onto place de la Concorde, the distinguished service, or the memorable wine list. ✉ *10 pl. de la Concorde,* ☎ *01–44–71–16–16. Reservations essential. Jacket and tie at dinner. AE, DC, MC, V. Métro: Concorde.*

$$$$ ✕ **Ledoyen.** Chef Ghislaine Arabian has set gastronomic fashion by concentrating on northern French cuisine and creating specialties with beer sauces, such as coquilles St-Jacques *à la bière* (cooked in beer). The elegant restaurant has gilded ceilings and walls, plush armchairs, and tables with candelabra. Luckily for those without an expense account, there's also a brasserie, Le Cercle Ledoyen; for about $50 a dinner (wine included) you can sample some of the daily specials. The brasserie is open on Saturdays; it's tucked underneath the main restaurant. ✉ *1 av. du Tuit, on the Carré des Champs-*

Elysées, ☎ *01–47–42–23–23. Reservations essential. AE, DC, MC, V. Closed weekends. Métro: Place de la Concorde or Champs-Elysées–Clemenceau.*

$$$$ ✕ **Pierre Gagnaire.** Legendary chef Pierre Gagnaire's
★ cooking is at once intellectual and poetic. Two intriguing dishes from a recent menu—it changes seasonally—included duck foie gras wrapped in bacon and lacquered like a Chinese duck, and sea bass smothered in herbs with tiny clams. The only drawbacks are the amateurish service and the puzzlingly brief wine list. ✉ *6 rue de Balzac,* ☎ *01–44–35–18–25. Reservations essential. AE, DC, MC, V. Closed Sun. Métro: Charles-de-Gaulle–Etoile.*

$$$$ ✕ **Taillevent.** Dining in the paneled rooms of this mid-19th-century mansion is nothing short of a sublime experience. Among the signature dishes are cream of watercress soup with caviar and truffled tart of game. Desserts are also superb, especially the creamy chocolate tart served with thyme ice cream. ✉ *15 rue Lamennais,* ☎ *01–45–63–39–94. Reservations 3–4 wks in advance essential. Jacket and tie. AE, MC, V. Closed weekends and Aug. Métro: Charles de Gaulle–Etoile.*

$$ ✕ **Androuet.** Ignore the airline-office decor and feast on the vast assortment of beautifully aged fromages at this famous temple to the cheeses of France. If you really love cheese, or just want to learn more about it, order the tasting menu, which will take you through the seven main French types. ✉ *41 rue d'Amsterdam,* ☎ *01–48–74–26–93. AE, DC, MC, V. Closed Sun. Métro: St-Lazare.*

$$ ✕ **La Fermette Marbeuf.** Prices here are exceptional, considering the excellent quality of the food, the surroundings, and the neighborhood. Try gâteau of chicken livers and sweetbreads, lamb *navarin* (stew with turnips and potatoes), and bitter chocolate fondant. ✉ *5 rue Marbeuf,* ☎ *01–47–20–63–53. AE, DC, MC, V. Métro: Franklin-D.-Roosevelt.*

$ ✕ **La Ferme St-Hubert.** The owner has a cheese shop next door—one of the best in the city—and from its shelves come the main ingredients for fondue, raclette, and the best *croque St-Hubert* (toasted cheese sandwich) in Paris. ✉ *21 rue Vignon,* ☎ *01–47–42–79–20. Reser-*

*vations essential at lunch. AE, MC, V. Closed Sun.
Métro: Madeleine.*

9ᵉ Arrondissement (Opéra)

$$ ✕ **Chez Jean.** This tiny, relaxed, off-the-beaten-path
★ place has been booked solid ever since it opened. Some
recent selections were a delicious cream of cèpes, John
Dory in a crust of potato, and luscious chocolate-and-
tea quenelles. ⊠ *52 rue Lamartine,* ☎ *01–48–78–
62–73. Reservations essential. MC, V. Closed Sun. No
lunch Sat. Métro: Cadet.*

10ᵉ Arrondissement
(République/Gare du Nord)

$$ ✕ **Brasserie Flo.** The first of brasserie king Jean-Paul
Bucher's Paris addresses is hard to find down its pas-
sageway near Gare de l'Est, but it's worth the effort. The
rich wood and stained glass is typically Alsatian, service
is enthusiastic, and brasserie standards such as shellfish,
steak tartare, and choucroute are mouthwatering. It's
open until 1:30 AM, with a special night-owl menu from
11 PM. ⊠ *7 cour des Petites Ecuries,* ☎ *01–47–70–
13–59. AE, DC, MC, V. Métro: Château d'Eau.*

$–$$ ✕ **Chez Michel.** If you're gastronomically intrepid—
★ willing to go out of your way for excellent food at fair
prices even if the decor and the out-of-the way neighborhood are drab—then this place is for you. Chef
Thierry Breton pulls a stylish crowd of Parisians with
his wonderful cuisine du marché and dishes from his native Brittany. Typical of Breton's kitchen are the lasagna
stuffed with chèvre cheese and the artichokes and tuna
steak with pureed peas. ⊠ *10 rue Belzunce,* ☎ *01–44–
53–06–20. Reservations essential. MC, V. Closed Sun.,
Mon. No lunch Sat. Métro: Gare du Nord.*

11ᵉ Arrondissement (Bastille/République)

$$ ✕ **Chardenoux.** A bit off the beaten track but well
worth the effort, this cozy neighborhood bistro attracts
a cross section of savvy Parisians. The traditional cook-
ing is first-rate: Start with one of the delicious salads,
such as the green beans and foie gras, and then sample
the veal chop with morels or a game dish. ⊠ *1 rue
Jules-Valles,* ☎ *01–43–71–49–52. AE, V. Closed week-
ends and Aug. Métro: Charonne.*

$ ✕ **Au Camelot.** Make a reservation the moment you get
★ to town if you want to be treated to chef Anne Desplanques's excellent, home-style cooking. A single, five-
course menu is served daily at this tiny 20-seat restaurant.
Desplanques trained with Christian Constant at the
Crillon Hotel, so expect creative dishes like crab lasagna
alongside classics like chicken in mushroom cream
sauce. ⊠ *50 rue Amelot,* ☎ *01–43–55–54–04. Reservations essential. No credit cards. Closed Sun. No lunch
Mon., Sat. Métro: République.*

$ ✕ **Jacques Mélac.** Robust cuisine matches noisy cama-
raderie at this popular wine bar–restaurant, owned by
mustachioed Jacques Mélac. Charcuterie, a salad of
preserved duck gizzards, braised beef, and cheeses from
central France are good choices. Monsieur Mélac, who
has a miniature vineyard out front, hosts a jolly party
at harvest time. ⊠ *42 rue Léon Frot,* ☎ *01–43–70–
59–27. MC, V. Closed weekends Aug. No dinner Mon.
Métro: Charonne.*

12ᵉ Arrondissement (Bastille/Gare de Lyon)

$$$ ✕ **Au Trou Gascon.** At this successful Belle Epoque es-
tablishment off the place Daumesnil, owner Alain Du-
tournier serves his version of the cuisine of Gascony—a
region of outstanding ham, foie gras, lamb, and poul-
try—and his classic white chocolate mousse. ⊠ *40 rue
Taine,* ☎ *01–43–44–34–26. AE, DC, MC, V. Closed
weekends, Christmas wk, and Aug. Métro: Daumesnil.*

$$$ ✕ **L'Oulette.** Chef-owner Marcel Baudis's take on the
★ cuisine of his native southwest France is original and de-
licious. Recommended dishes include oxtail with foie
gras, fresh cod with celeriac and walnuts, and *pain
d'épices* (spice cake). The restaurant, in the rebuilt Bercy
district, is a bit hard to find, so bring your map. ⊠ *15
pl. Lachambeaudie,* ☎ *01–40–02–02–12. AE, MC, V.
Closed Sun. No lunch Sat. Métro: Dugommier.*

$ ✕ **Les Zygomates.** This handsome old butcher's shop
converted into a bistro is in a part of the city few tourists
venture to, so it's mostly filled with Parisians. Experience delicious modern bistro food, like a terrine of rabbit with tarragon, chicken in cream with chives, and a
very fairly priced catch-of-the-day selection. ⊠ *7 rue
Capri,* ☎ *01–40–19–93–04. V. Closed Sun., Sat.*

June–Sept., 1st 3 wks of Aug. No lunch Sat. Oct.–May. Métro: Michel-Bizot, Daumesnil.

13e Arrondissement (Les Gobelins)

$$$ ✕ **Au Petit Marguéry.** Both staff and diners seem to be having a good time in this warm, convivial place. The menu goes beyond the usual bistro classics to include such dishes as cold lobster, cod fillet with spices, and excellent lamb of the Pyrénées. Prices are at the low end of this category. ⊠ *9 bd. de Port Royal,* ☎ *01–43–31–58–59. AE, DC, MC, V. Closed Sun., Mon., Christmas wk, and Aug. Métro: Les Gobelins.*

$$ ✕ **Anacreon.** A former chef from the Tour d'Argent has transformed a neighborhood café into a pleasant new-wave bistro serving inventive dishes such as pumpkin soup garnished with bacon and chorizo sausage or snails in a watercress cream sauce. ⊠ *53 bd. St-Marcel,* ☎ *01–43–31–71–18. Reservations essential. MC, V. Closed Sat., Sun. Métro: Les Gobelins.*

14e Arrondissement (Montparnasse)

$$$$ ✕ **Montparnasse 25.** Chef Jean-Yves Guého's stint in Hong Kong gave him a mastery of Chinese cuisine, which he has applied to classical French cooking with intriguing results. The spectacular roast piglet, for example, is served in two courses—the rack and haunch rolled in sesame seeds with a sate sauce and the ribs and shoulder with Asian vegetables. Don't miss the cheese course—there are more than 150 to choose from, all explained by a *maître fromager.* ⊠ *19 rue Commandant-Mouchotte,* ☎ *01–44–36–44–25. AE, DC, MC, V. Closed weekends. Métro: Montparnasse.*

$$ ✕ **La Coupole.** This world-renowned, cavernous address in Montparnasse practically defines the term brasserie (it's owned by Jean-Paul Bucher). Despite noise and crowds, it has been popular with everyone from Left Bank intellectuals (Jean-Paul Sartre and Simone de Beauvoir were regulars) to bourgeois grandmothers. Expect the usual brasserie menu, including perhaps the largest shellfish presentation in Paris, choucroute, and a wide range of desserts. The buffet breakfast from 7:30 to 10:30 daily is an excellent value. ⊠ *102 bd. du Montparnasse,* ☎ *01–43–20–14–20. AE, DC, MC, V. Métro: Vavin.*

$ ✕ **La Régalade.** Although it's in a remote, colorless residential neighborhood, which is a nuisance, Yves Camdeborde's cooking is worth the trip. A veteran of the Crillon, he has, remarkably, kept prices low—$37 for a three-course feast. Tables need to be booked at least one month in advance, but service continues until midnight, and you can often sneak in late in the evening. ⊠ *49 av. Jean-Moulin,* ☎ *01–45–45–68–58. MC, V. Closed Sun., Mon., and Aug. No lunch Sat. Métro: Alesia.*

15e Arrondissement (Motte-Picquet/Balard)

$$ ✕ **La Dinée.** Up-and-coming chef Christophe Chabanel's restaurant in this rather remote location is filled noon and night by a crowd of stylish regulars who come to be surprised by his culinary creativity. Signature dishes include fillet of sole with baby shrimp and chicken medallions with peppers in a corn vinaigrette. ⊠ *85 rue Leblanc,* ☎ *01–45–54–20–49. V. Closed weekends. Métro: Balard.*

$$ ✕ **Philippe Detourbe.** With its black-lacquer trim, mir-
★ rors, and burgundy velvet upholstery, this place is unexpectedly glamorous. It also serves spectacular food for remarkably good prices, so book several days in advance. Detourbe, a self-taught chef, is extremely gifted and very ambitious—dishes may include smoked salmon filled with cabbage *rémoulade* (creamy dressing) or cod steak with white beans and caramelized endives. ⊠ *8 rue Nicholas Charlet,* ☎ *01–42–19–08–59. Reservations essential. MC, V. Closed Sun. No lunch Sat. Métro: Pasteur.*

16e Arrondissement (Trocadéro/Bois de Boulogne)

$$$$ ✕ **Alain Ducasse.** Since he took over from Joel Robu-
★ chon, Ducasse has surprised everyone by serving resolutely classical French dishes. One does not feel, however, that this is the pinnacle of French dining, as one did with Joel Robuchon. Ducasse is a marvelous cook, but dishes like a pastry case filled with mushrooms, shrimps, and frog's legs or duckling steamed with anise, satisfy rather than excite. Still you can get a solidly luxurious meal, though you'll have to forgive the robotlike service and the staggeringly expensive menu; the 480-franc lunch

menu is your best bet. ⊠ *59 av. Raymond-Poincare,* ☎ *01–47–27–12–27. Reservations several months in advance essential. AE, DC, MC, V. Closed Sat., Sun. Métro: Victor Hugo.*

$$$ ✕ **Jamin.** At this intimate, elegant restaurant, where Joel
★ Robuchon made his name, you can find excellent, haute cuisine at almost half the price of what you'd find elsewhere. Benoit Guichard, Robuchon's second for many years, is a subtle and accomplished chef and a particularly brilliant *saucier* (sauce maker). The menu changes regularly, but Guichard tends toward dishes like ginger-spiked salad with squid and crayfish, and braised beef with cumin-scented carrots. The poached pears with spice-bread ice cream makes an excellent dessert. ⊠ *32 rue de Longchamp,* ☎ *01–45–53–00–07. Reservations essential. AE, DC, MC, V. Closed Sat., Sun. Métro: Iéna.*

$$–$$$ ✕ **Prunier.** Founded in 1925, this seafood restaurant is one of the best—and surely the prettiest—in Paris. The famous Art Deco mosaics glitter and the white marble counters shine with the impeccably fresh shellfish displayed like jewels. The kitchen not only excels at classic French fish cooking but has added some interesting dishes, like a *Saintongeaise* plate—raw oysters with grilled sausages. No reservations are needed for the raw bar on the main level, but book for lunch or dinner in the upstairs dining room. ⊠ *16 av. Victor Hugo,* ☎ *01–44–17–35–85. Jacket and tie. AE, DC, MC, V. Closed Sun., Mon. Métro: Etoile.*

$$ ✕ **La Butte Chaillot.** A dramatic iron staircase connects two levels decorated in turquoise and earth colors at the latest, largest, and most impressive of star chef Guy Savoy's fashionable bistros. Dining here is part theater, but it's not all show: The menu includes tasty ravioli and stuffed veal breast with rosemary. ⊠ *112 av. Kléber,* ☎ *01–47–27–88–88. AE, MC, V. Métro: Trocadéro.*

$$ ✕ **Le Relais du Parc.** This bistro-annex is now run by
★ Alain Ducasse, who has instituted a wonderful, new menu that allows you to eat as large or light as you like. Two delicious starters—the lobster salad and the baby potatoes with black truffles in a creamy oxtail-stock sauce—make good meals, followed by cheese or dessert. Watch out for high prices on the wine list. ⊠ *55 av. Raymond-*

Poincaré, ☎ *01–44–05–66–10. Reservations essential. AE, DC, MC, V. Métro: Victor Hugo.*

$ ✕ **Le Petit Rétro.** Come to this immaculate little bistro when you want a good solid meal, like the perfect *pavé de boeuf* (thick steak) in a ruddy red-wine and stock sauce, accompanied by potatoes au gratin and caramelized braised endive. ⊠ *5 rue Mesnil,* ☎ *01–44–05–06–05. MC, V. Closed Sun. No lunch Mon. Métro: Victor Hugo.*

17e Arrondissement (Monceau/Clichy)

$$$$ ✕ **Amphyclès.** At this much-anticipated restaurant, chef-owner Philippe Groult has not disappointed. His exciting menu includes cauliflower soup with caviar, herb salad, and duck with coriander and orange. Amphyclès is one of the few grand Parisian restaurants still to proffer desserts from a pastry trolley. ⊠ *78 av. des Ternes,* ☎ *01–40–68–01–01. AE, DC, MC, V. Reservations essential 1 wk in advance. Closed Sun. No lunch Sat. Métro: Ternes.*

$$$$ ✕ **Guy Savoy.** Top chef Guy Savoy's other five bistros
★ have not distracted him too much from his handsome luxury restaurant near the Arc de Triomphe. The oysters in aspic, sea bass with spices, and poached and grilled pigeon reveal the magnitude of his talent. His millefeuille is a contemporary classic. ⊠ *18 rue Troyon,* ☎ *01–43–80–40–61. AE, MC, V. Closed Sun. No lunch Sat. Métro: Charles de Gaulle–Etoile.*

$$–$$$ ✕ **Au Petit Colombier.** It's a perennial favorite among Parisians, who come to eat comforting *cuisine bourgeoise* in the warm dining rooms accented with wood and bright copper. Menu standards include milk-fed lamb chop *en cocotte* (in a small, enameled casserole) and coq au vin. Service is friendly and unpretentious. It's open for Sunday dinner. ⊠ *42 rue des Acacias,* ☎ *01–43–80–28–54. AE, MC, V. Closed Sat. No lunch Sun. Métro: Charles de Gaulle–Etoile.*

$$ ✕ **Le Timgad.** Do some gustatory exploring at this elegant, beautifully decorated North African restaurant. Start with a savory *brick* (crispy parchment pastry filled with meat, eggs, or seafood), followed by succulent *tagine* (meat or poultry that's slowly braised inside a domed pottery casserole). Lamb tagine with artichokes

is especially good. ⊠ *21 rue de Brunel,* ☎ *01–45–74– 23–70. MC, V. Métro: Argentine.*

$ ✕ **L'Huitrier.** If you share the Parisians' craving for oysters, this is the place for you. Owner Alain Bunel will describe the different kinds available; you can follow these with any of several fish specials offered daily. ⊠ *16 rue Saussier-Leroy,* ☎ *01–40–54–83–44. AE, MC, V. Métro: Ternes.*

18ᵉ Arrondissement (Montmartre)

$$$$ ✕ **A. Beauvilliers.** Pickwickian owner Edouard Carlier is a born party-giver, and his flower-filled, lavishly decorated restaurant is fittingly festive. A tiny, vine-covered terrace makes for delightful summer dining. Recommended are the red mullet *en escabèche* (in a peppery marinade) and foie gras, lobster, and sweetbread tourte. The mouth-puckering lemon tart is not to be missed. One drawback: Service can be distant. ⊠ *52 rue Lamarck,* ☎ *01–42–54–54–42. Reservations essential. Jacket required. AE, MC, V. Closed Sun. No lunch Mon. Métro: Lamarck-Caulaincourt.*

$ ✕ **Le Restaurant.** This pleasant little restaurant remains an oasis in a neighborhood where it's not easy to find a good meal. The prix-fixe menu features his inventive approach to bistro cooking, using Asian and African seasoning to brighten up classical dishes. The menu changes regularly, but dishes like guinea hen with preserved lemon and duckling with figs express his style. ⊠ *32 rue Veron,* ☎ *01–42–23–06–22. AE, MC, V. Closed Mon. Métro: Abbesses.*

19ᵉ Arrondissement (Buttes Chaumont/La Villette)

$$ ✕ **La Verriere.** This simply-decorated little place is a ster-
★ ling example of a price-conscious, market-menu bistro. Chef Eric Frechon worked with Christian Constant at the Crillon, which means his cooking is more adventurous than most bistro fare. Examples of his dishes include mackerel stuffed with celery rémoulade and thick slabs of bacon "lacquered" with spices and served on a bed of pickled turnips. ⊠ *10 rue du Général-Brunet,* ☎ *01– 40–40–03–30. V. Closed Sat., Sun. Métro: Danube.*

Cafés

Cafés are found at every bend in Paris—you may prefer a posh perch at a renowned *café littéraire* (literary cafés), where *intellectuels* such as Hemingway, de Beauvoir, and Sartre wrote some of their greatest works, or opt for a seat at a tiny *café de quartier* (neighborhood café), where locals come to discuss politics and gossip. Following is a list of cafés that will give you a feel for Paris's best.

1er Arrondissement (Les Halles/Palais-Royal)

Au Père Tranquille. One of the best places for people-watching, this café also offers free entertainment from street artists and local performers. ⊠ *16 rue Pierre Lescot,* ☎ *01– 45–08–00–34. Métro Les Halles.*

Le Ruc Univers. Actors from the Comédie Française hang out at this elegant and rather pricey brasserie dating from 1925. ⊠ *1 pl. André Malraux,* ☎ *01–42–60–31–57. Métro Palais-Royal.*

4e Arrondissement (Marais/Beaubourg/Ile St-Louis)

Le Flore en l'Ile. At this café on the Ile St-Louis you can find renowned Berthillon ice cream and a magnificent view of the Seine. ⊠ *42 quai d'Orléans,* ☎ *01–43–29–88–27. Métro Pont Marie.*

Le Loir dans la Théière. This wonderful tea shop in the heart of the Marais has comfortable armchairs and delicious patisseries. ⊠ *3 rue des Rosiers,* ☎ *01–42–72–90–61. Métro St-Paul.*

Ma Bourgogne. On the exquisite place des Vosges, this is a calm oasis for a coffee or a light lunch away from the noisy streets. ⊠ *19 pl. des Vosges,* ☎ *01–42–78–44–64. Métro St-Paul.*

Mariage Frères. London isn't the only city with outstanding tea shops: This elegant place serves 500 kinds of tea, along with delicious tarts. ⊠ *30 rue du Bourg-Tibourg,* ☎ *01–42–72–28–11. Métro Hôtel-de-Ville.*

6e Arrondissement (St-Germain/Montparnasse)

Brasserie Lipp. This brasserie, with its turn-of-the-century decor, was a favorite spot of Hemingway's; today television celebrities, journalists, and politicians come here regularly. ⊠ *151 bd. St-Germain,* ☎ *01–45–48–53–91. Métro St-Germain-des-Prés.*

Café des Deux Magots. Dubbed the second home of the "*élite intellectuelle,*" this café counted Rimbaud, Verlaine, Mallarmé, Wilde, and the Surrealists among its regulars. ⊠ *170 bd. St-Germain,* ☎ *01–45–48–55–25. Métro St-Germain-des-Prés.*

Café de Flore. Picasso, Chagall, Sartre, and de Beauvoir, attracted by the luxury of a heated café, worked and wrote here in the early 20th century. Today you'll find more tourists than intellectuals, but its outdoor terrace is still a popular spot. ⊠ *172 bd. St-Germain,* ☎ *01–45–48–55–26. Métro St-Germain-des-Prés.*

Café de la Mairie. Preferred by Henry Miller and Saul Bellow to those on the noisy boulevard St-Germain, this place still retains the quiet and unpretentious air of a local café. ⊠ *8 pl. St-Sulpice,* ☎ *01–43–26–67–82. Métro St-Sulpice.*

La Rotonde. Once a second home to foreign artists and political exiles in the '20s and '30s, the café's clientele isn't as exotic today. But it's still a pleasant place to have a coffee on the sunny terrace. ⊠ *105 bd. Montparnasse,* ☎ *01–43–26–68–84. Métro Montparnasse.*

Le Sélect. Isadora Duncan and Hart Crane used to hang out here; now it's a popular spot for a post-cinema beer. ⊠ *99 bd. Montparnasse,* ☎ *01–45–48–38–24. Métro Vavin.*

8ᵉ Arrondissement (Champs-Elysées)

Le Fouquet's. At one of James Joyce's and Orson Welles's favorite cafés, brass plaques bear their names, as well as those of other famous patrons. ⊠ *99 av. des Champs-Elysées,* ☎ *01–47–23–70–60. Métro George-V.*

14ᵉ Arrondissement (Montparnasse)

Café du Dôme. Now a fancy brasserie, this place began as a dingy meeting place for exiled artists and intellectuals such as Lenin, Picasso, and Chaim Soutine. ⊠ *108 bd. Montparnasse,* ☎ *01–43–35–25–81. Métro Vavin.*

18ᵉ Arrondissement (Montmartre)

La Crémaillère. Alphonse Mucha frescoes decorate the walls at this veritable monument to fin-de-siècle art. ⊠ *15 pl. du Tertre,* ☎ *01–46–06–58–59. Métro Anvers.*

4 Lodging

Updated
by
Suzanne
Rowan
Kelleher

WINDING STAIRCASES, flower-filled window boxes, concierges who seem to have stepped from a 19th-century novel—all of these still exist in abundance in Paris hotels. So do grand rooms with marble baths, Belle Epoque lobbies, and a polished staff at your beck and call. In Paris there are wonderful hotels for every taste and budget. The Paris Tourist Office's annual lodging guide lists 1,498 member hotels in the city's 20 arrondissements. The true count, though, is closer to 2,000—some 80,000 rooms in all.

Our criteria when selecting the hotels reviewed below were quality, location, and character. Few chain hotels are listed, since they frequently lack the charm and authenticity found in typical Parisian lodgings. (Best Western is a notable exception.) Similarly, we list fewer hotels in outlying arrondissements (the 10ᵉ to the 20ᵉ) because these are farther from the major sites. Generally, there are more Right Bank hotels offering luxury—or at any rate formality—than there are on the Left Bank, where hotels are frequently smaller and richer in old-fashioned charm. The Right Bank's 1ᵉʳ and 8ᵉ arrondissements are still the most exclusive and prices here reflect this. Less-expensive alternatives on the Right Bank are the fashionable Marais quarter (3ᵉ and 4ᵉ arrondissements) and the 11ᵉ and 12ᵉ, near the Opéra Bastille.

Despite the huge choice of hotels, you should always reserve well in advance, especially if you're determined to stay in a specific place. You can do this by telephoning ahead, then writing or faxing for confirmation. Be sure to discuss refund policies before making a deposit. During peak seasons, some hotels require total prepayment. Always demand written confirmation of your reservation, detailing the duration of your stay, the price, the location and the type of your room (single or double, twin beds or double), and the bathroom (☞ *below*).

As part of a general upgrade of the city's hotels in recent years, scores of lackluster, shabby Paris lodgings have been replaced by good-value establishments in the lower to middle price ranges. Despite widespread improvements, however, many Paris hotels still have idiosyncrasies—some charming, others less so. Hotel rooms in Paris's oldest quarters are generally much smaller than their American counterparts. The standard French double bed is slightly smaller than the American version. Although air-conditioning has become de rigueur in middle- to higher-priced hotels, it is generally not a prerequisite for comfort. (Paris's hot-weather season doesn't last long.) All rooms and suites include full bath facilities, including *baignoire* (tub) or *douche* (shower); any exceptions are noted. It's increasingly rare to find moderately priced places that offer shared toilets or bathrooms down the hall, but make sure you know what you are getting when you book.

Almost all Paris hotels charge extra for breakfast, with prices ranging from 30 francs to more than 195 francs per person in luxury establishments. Though hotels may not automatically add the breakfast charge to your bill, it's wise to inform the desk staff if you don't plan to have breakfast there. For anything more than the standard Continental breakfast of café au lait and baguette or croissants, the price will be higher.

You'll notice that stars appear on a shield on the facade of most hotels. The French government grades hotels on a scale from one star to four-star deluxe based on a notoriously complicated evaluation of amenities and services. You can expect two- and three-star hotels to have private bathrooms, elevators, and in-room televisions. At the high end are the luxurious four-star hotels, which have excellent amenities and prices to match. The ratings are sometimes misleading, however, since many hotels prefer to be under starred for tax reasons.

We list hotels by price. Often a hotel in a certain price category will have a few rooms that are less expensive; it's worth asking. Rates must be posted in all rooms (usually on the backs of doors), with all extra charges clearly shown. There is a nominal *séjour* tax of 7 francs per person, per night.

Unless otherwise stated, the hotels reviewed below have elevators, rooms have TVs (many with cable, including CNN), minibars, and telephones, and English is spoken.

Additional facilities, such as restaurants and health clubs, are listed at the end of each review.

CATEGORY	COST*
$$$$	over 1,750 frs.
$$$	1,000 frs.–1,750 frs.
$$	600 frs.–1,000 frs.
$	under 600 frs.

All prices are for a standard double room, including tax and service.

1er Arrondissement (Louvre)

$$$$ ⊡ **Costes.** Jean-Louis and Gilbert Costes's eponymous
★ hotel is easily their most ambitious project to date. The first surprise is the departure from postmodernism that has been their hallmark. Instead, this sumptuous hotel conjures up the palaces of Napoléon III. Every room is swathed in rich garnet and bronze tones and contains a luxurious mélange of patterned fabrics, heavy swags, and enough brocade and fringe to blanket the Champs-Elysées. The bathrooms are truly marvelous affairs. ⊠ *239 rue St-Honoré, 75001,* ☎ *01–42–44–50–50,* FAX *01–42–44–50–01. 85 rooms. Restaurant, bar, air-conditioning, in-room modem lines, in-room safes, no-smoking rooms, room service, indoor pool, sauna, exercise room, laundry service. AE, DC, MC, V. Métro: Tuileries.*

$$$$ ⊡ **Inter-Continental.** This exquisite late-19th-century hotel has just completed an ambitious restoration. The building was designed by the architect of the Paris Opéra, Charles Garnier, and three of its gilt and stuccoed public rooms are official historic monuments. Spacious guest rooms overlook quiet inner courtyards. Service is impeccable. ⊠ *3 rue de Castiglione, 75001,* ☎ *01–44–77–11–11, 800/327–0200 in the U.S.,* FAX *01–44–77–10–10. 450 rooms and 75 suites. Restaurant, bar, air-conditioning, in-room safes, no-smoking rooms, room service, laundry service, meeting rooms. AE, DC, MC, V. Métro: Concorde.*

$$$$ ⊡ **Ritz.** Surrounded by the city's finest jewelers, the Ritz is the crowning gem of the sparkling place Vendôme. Festooned with gilt and ormolu and dripping with crystal chandeliers, this dazzling hotel is the epitome of fin-de-siècle Paris. Yet it's surprisingly intimate. The lack of a lobby discourages paparazzi and sightseers who might annoy the privileged clientele. Legendary suites are named after former residents, such as Marcel Proust and Coco Chanel. Don't miss the famous Hemingway Bar (which the writer claimed to have "liberated" in 1944). ⊠ *15 pl. Vendôme, 75001,* ☏ *01−43−16−30−30,* FAX *01−43−16−36−68. 142 rooms and 45 suites. 3 restaurants, 2 bars, air-conditioning, in-room safes, room service, indoor pool, beauty salon, health club, shops, laundry service, meeting rooms, parking (fee). AE, DC, MC, V. Métro: Opéra.*

$$ 🔛 **Britannique.** Open since 1870, the three-star Britannique blends courteous English service with old-fashioned French elegance. It has retained its handsome winding staircase and offers well-appointed, soundproof rooms done in chic, warm tones. ⊠ *20 av. Victoria, 75001,* ☏ *01−42−33−74−59,* FAX *01−42−33−82−65. 31 rooms with bath, 9 with shower. Bar, in-room safes. AE, DC, MC, V. Métro: Châtelet.*

$ 🔛 **Louvre Forum.** This friendly two-star hotel is a find: ★ Smack in the center of town, it offers clean, comfortable, well-equipped rooms (with satellite TV) at extremely reasonable prices. The inexpensive breakfast is served in a homey vaulted cellar. ⊠ *25 rue du Bouloi, 75001,* ☏ *01−42−36−54−19,* FAX *01−42−33−66−31. 11 rooms with bath, 16 with shower. Bar. AE, DC, MC, V. Métro: Louvre.*

2ᵉ Arrondissement (Le Bourse)

$$ 🔛 **Gaillon-Opéra.** One of the most charming in the Opéra neighborhood, this hotel has so much character that you would never guess that it's part of a chain. But Best Western has wonderfully preserved the building's original atmosphere: It still has its old oak beams, stone walls, marble tiles, and leafy patio. ⊠ *9 rue Gaillon, 75002,* ☏ *01−47−42−47−74, 800/528−1234 in the U.S.,* FAX *01−47−42−01−23. 26 rooms and 2 suites. Bar, air-conditioning, in-room modem lines, in-room safes, no-smoking rooms, room service, baby-sitting, laundry service. AE, DC, MC, V. Métro: Opéra.*

$$ ⌘ **Hôtel de Noailles.** With a nod to the work of post-
★ modern designers like André Putnam and Philippe
Starck, this new-wave inn is a star among Paris's new
crop of well-priced, style-driven boutique hotels. Rooms
are individually decorated with funky furnishings and
contemporary details; breakfast is included in the rate.
✉ *9 rue de Michodière, 75002,* ☎ *01–47–42–92–90,*
FAX *01–49–24–92–71. 48 rooms with bath, 5 with
shower. In-room safes, no-smoking rooms, laundry ser-
vice. AE, MC, V. Métro: Opéra.*

3e Arrondissement (Marais)

$$$$ ⌘ **Pavillon de la Reine.** This magnificent mansion, re-
★ constructed from original plans, is on the 17th-century
place des Vosges. It's filled with Louis XIII–style fire-
places and antiques. Ask for a duplex with French win-
dows overlooking the first of two flower-filled courtyards
behind the historic Queen's Pavilion. Breakfast is served
in a vaulted cellar. ✉ *28 pl. des Vosges, 75003,* ☎ *01–
42–77–96–40, 800/447–7462 in the U.S.,* FAX *01–42–
77–63–06. 30 rooms and 25 suites. Bar, breakfast
room, air-conditioning, room service, laundry service,
free parking. AE, DC, MC, V. Métro: Bastille, St-Paul,
Chemin Vert.*

4e Arrondissement (Marais/Ile St-Louis)

$$ ⌘ **Caron de Beaumarchais.** The theme of this intimate
★ jewel is the work of Caron de Beaumarchais, who wrote
the *Marriage of Figaro* in 1778. First-edition copies of
his books adorn the public spaces. Rooms are faithfully
decorated to reflect the taste of 18th-century French nobility, right down to the reproduction wallpapers and up-
holsteries. Fresh flowers and fluffy bathrobes are a bonus
for the price. The fifth- and sixth-floor rooms with bal-
conies are the largest and have wonderful views across
Right Bank rooftops. ✉ *12 rue Vieille-du-Temple, 75004,*
☎ *01–42–72–34–12,* FAX *01–42–72–34–63. 17 rooms
with bath, 2 with shower. Air-conditioning, in-room
safes, laundry service. AE, DC, MC, V. Métro: Hôtel de
Ville.*

$$ ⊞ **Deux-Iles.** This converted 17th-century mansion on the Ile St-Louis has long won plaudits for charm and comfort. The delightful rooms, blessed with exposed beams, are small but fresh and airy. Ask for one overlooking the little garden courtyard. In winter, a roaring fire warms the lounge. ⊠ *59 rue St-Louis-en-l'Ile, 75004,* ☎ *01–43–26–13–35,* FAX *01–43–29–60–25. 8 rooms with bath, 9 with shower. Air-conditioning, in-room safes, no-smoking rooms, laundry service, meeting rooms. AE, MC, V. Métro: Pont-Marie.*

$
★ ⊞ **Castex.** This two-star Marais hotel in a Revolution-era building is a bargain-hunter's dream. Rooms are low on frills but squeaky clean, the owners are extremely friendly, and the prices are rock-bottom, which ensures that the hotel is often booked months ahead by a largely American clientele. There's no elevator, and the only TV is in the ground-floor salon. ⊠ *5 rue Castex, 75004,* ☎ *01–42–72–31–52,* FAX *01–42–72–57–91. 4 rooms with bath, 23 with shower. MC, V. Métro: Bastille.*

$ ⊞ **Hôtel du 7ᵉ Art.** The theme of this hip Marais hotel fits its name ("Seventh Art" is what the French call filmmaking): Hollywood from the '40s to the '60s. Posters of Cagney, Marilyn, Chaplin, and their contemporaries cover the walls. Rooms are small and spartan, but clean, quiet, and equipped with cable TV. There's no elevator. ⊠ *20 rue St-Paul, 75004,* ☎ *01–42–77–04–03,* FAX *01–42–77–69–10. 9 rooms with bath, 14 with shower. Bar, breakfast room, in-room safes. AE, DC, MC, V. Métro: St-Paul.*

5ᵉ Arrondissement (Latin Quarter)

$$
★ ⊞ **Jardin du Luxembourg.** Blessed with a charming staff and a smart, stylish look, this hotel is on a calm side street just a block from the Luxembourg Gardens. Rooms are a bit small (common for this neighborhood) but intelligently furnished and warmly decorated in ocher, rust, and indigo à la provençale. Ask for one with a balcony overlooking the street; the best, No. 25, has dormer windows and a peekaboo view of the Eiffel Tower. ⊠ *5 Impasse Royer-Collard, 75005,* ☎ *01–40–46–08–88,* FAX *01–40–46–02–28. 23 rooms with*

bath, 2 with shower. Bar, air-conditioning, in-room safes. AE, DC, MC, V. Métro: Luxembourg.

$ **Familia.** The hospitable Gaucheron family bend over
★   backward for their guests and it's hard to beat this level
of homespun comfort for the price. Some rooms feature
romantic sepia frescoes of celebrated Paris scenes that
were painted by an artist from the Beaux Arts; others
are appointed with exquisite Louis XV–style furnishings.
Those overlooking the animated Latin Quarter street have
double-glazed windows; book ahead for one with a
walk-out balcony on the second or fifth floor. *11 rue
des Ecoles, 75005,* ☎ *01–43–54–55–27,* FAX *01–43–
29–61–77. 14 rooms with bath, 16 with shower. AE,
MC, V. Métro: Cardinal Lemoine.*

$ **Grandes Écoles.** This delightfully intimate two-star
place looks and feels like a country cottage dropped
smack in the middle of the Latin Quarter. It is off the
street and occupies three buildings on a beautiful leafy
garden, where breakfast is served in summer. Parquet
floors, Louis-Philippe furnishings, lace bedspreads, and
the absence of TV all add to the rustic ambience. *75
rue du Cardinal Lemoine, 75005,* ☎ *01–43–26–79–
23,* FAX *01–43–25–28–15. 45 rooms with bath, 6 with
shower. No-smoking rooms. MC, V. Métro: Cardinal
Lemoine.*

6ᵉ Arrondissement (St-Germain/Montparnasse)

$$$$ **Relais Christine.** On a quiet street between the Seine
and boulevard St-Germain, this luxurious and popular
Left Bank hotel, occupying 16th-century abbey cloisters,
oozes romantic ambience. Rooms are spacious (particularly the duplexes on the upper floors) and well appointed in the old Parisian style; the best have exposed
beams and overlook the garden. The breakfast room is
an erstwhile stone chapel. *3 rue Christine, 75006,* ☎
01–43–26–71–80, FAX *01–43–26–89–38. 35 rooms
and 16 suites. Bar, air-conditioning, room service, baby-
sitting, laundry service, meeting rooms, free parking. AE,
DC, MC, V. Métro: Odéon.*

$$$–$$$$ **L'Hôtel.** Rock idols and movie stars adore this ex-
pensive and eccentric Left Bank hotel. Oscar Wilde died

here in Room 16. The decor is over the top at times; one small double is decorated entirely in leopard skin; another handsome suite features the mirrored, Art Deco boudoir furniture of vaudeville star Mistinguett. Be sure to ask about your room's size; many are extremely small. ⊠ *13 rue des Beaux-Arts, 75006,* ☎ *01–44–41–99–00,* FAX *01–43–25–64–81. 14 rooms and 2 suites with bath, 10 rooms with shower. Bar, air-conditioning, in-room safes, laundry service. AE, DC, MC, V. Métro: St-Germain-des-Prés.*

$$$ 🚇 **Relais St-Germain.** The interior-designer owners of
★   this outstanding hotel in the heart of St-Germain-des-Prés have exquisite taste and a superb respect for tradition and detail. Moreover, the rooms are at least twice the size of what you'll find at other hotels in the area for the same price. Doubles have separate sitting areas; four have kitchenettes. Breakfast is included in the rate. ⊠ *9 carrefour de l'Odéon, 75006,* ☎ *01–43–29–12–05,* FAX *01–46–33–45–30. 21 rooms and 1 suite. Breakfast room, wine bar, air-conditioning, in-room safes, room service, baby-sitting, laundry service. AE, DC, MC, V. Métro: Odéon.*

$$–$$$ 🚇 **Hôtel de L'Abbaye.** This delightful hotel near St-Sulpice, in the heart of the Left Bank, was a convent in the 18th century. It has a stone-vaulted entrance, and the first-floor rooms open onto a flower-filled garden. Some rooms on the top floor have oak beams and alcoves, and there are four duplexes with private terraces. Breakfast is included. ⊠ *10 rue Cassette, 75006,* ☎ *01–45–44–38–11,* FAX *01–45–48–07–86. 42 rooms and 4 suites. Bar, breakfast room, air-conditioning, room service. AE, MC, V. Métro: St-Sulpice.*

$$–$$$ 🚇 **Relais St-Sulpice.** The decor in this stylish spot is a blend of various periods and regions—Provençal tiles adorn the bathrooms; Chinese engravings wink to Parisians' penchant for the Orient in the 1930s; and thick, cotton-pique downy comforters envelop wrought-iron beds. There's a sauna downstairs, right off the atrium breakfast salon. ⊠ *3 rue Garancière, 75006,* ☎ *01–46–33–99–00,* FAX *01–46–33–00–10. 26 rooms. Air-conditioning, in-room modem lines, in-room safes,*

Paris Lodging

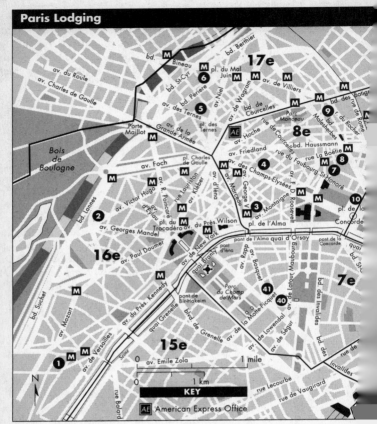

KEY

AE American Express Office

L'Astor, **8**
Atelier
Montparnasse, **37**
Le Bristol, **7**
Britannique, **26**
Caron de
Beaumarchais, **20**
Castex, **23**

Champ de
Mars, **41**
Costes, **13**
Crillon, **10**
Deux-Iles, **25**
Ermitage, **19**
Etoile-Péreire, **6**
Familia, **27**

Gaillon-Opéra, **16**
Grand Hôtel
Inter-
Continental, **14**
Grandes
Écoles, **28**
L'Hôtel, **30**
Hôtel de
L'Abbaye, **38**

Hôtel de
Noailles, **15**
Hôtel du
7e Art, **24**
Inter-
Continental, **12**
Istria, **35**
Jardin du
Luxembourg, **33**

*no-smoking rooms, sauna, meeting rooms, parking (fee).
AE, DC, MC, V. Métro: Mabillon, St-Sulpice.*

$$ ⊞ **Atelier Montparnasse.** This Art Deco–inspired gem
★ of a hotel was designed with style and comfort in mind.
Rooms are tastefully decorated and spacious and all the
bathrooms feature mosaic reproductions of famous
French paintings. The hotel is well situated in Mont-
parnasse within walking distance of the Luxembourg
Gardens and St-Germain-des-Prés. ⊠ *49 rue Vavin,
75006,* ☎ *01–46–33–60–00,* ℻ *01–40–51–04–21.
16 rooms and 1 triple. Bar, room service, laundry ser-
vice. AE, DC, MC, V. Métro: Vavin.*

7ᵉ Arrondissement (Invalides/École Militaire)

$$$–$$$$ ⊞ **Montalembert.** The Montalembert, a creation of
★ hotel goddess Grace Leo-Andrieu, is one of Paris's most
original boutique hotels. A host of signature elements
were designed for the hotel by the world's hippest de-
signers: Frette linens and fabrics, Cascais marble bath-
rooms, and cast-bronze door handles. Ask about special
packages if you're staying for more than three nights.
⊠ *3 rue de Montalembert, 75007,* ☎ *01–45–49–68–
68, 800/447–7462 in the U.S.,* ℻ *01–45–49–69–49.
41 rooms and 5 suites with bath, 10 rooms with shower.
Restaurant, bar, air-conditioning, in-room safes, room
service, in-room VCRs, baby-sitting, laundry service,
meeting rooms. AE, DC, MC, V. Métro: Rue du Bac.*

$$–$$$ ⊞ **Le Tourville.** Here is a rare find: an intimate four-star
hotel at more affordable prices. Each room has crisp,
virgin-white damask upholstery set against pastel or
ocher walls, original artwork, and fabulous old mirrors.
Though most doubles are priced at the low end of the
$$ category, the four doubles with lovely walk-out ter-
races nip into the $$$ bracket. ⊠ *16 av. de Tourville,
75007,* ☎ *01–47–05–62–62, 800/528–3549 in the
U.S.,* ℻ *01–47–05–43–90. 28 rooms and 2 junior
suites. Bar, air-conditioning, laundry service. AE, DC,
MC, V. Métro: École Militaire.*

$ ⊞ **Champ de Mars.** Françoise and Stéphane Gourdal's
★ comfortable hotel has rooms done in an attractive blue-
and-yellow French country-house style. All are equipped

with satellite TV and CNN. The two on the ground floor open onto a leafy courtyard. The neighborhood—near the Eiffel Tower and Invalides—is also difficult to beat. ✉ *7 rue du Champ de Mars, 75007,* ☎ *01–45–51–52–30,* FAX *01–45–51–64–36. 19 rooms with bath, 6 with shower. AE, MC, V. Métro: École Militaire.*

8ᵉ Arrondissement (Champs-Elysées)

$$$$ 🏨 **L'Astor.** Following a top-to-bottom makeover, L'Astor has been reborn as a bastion of highly stylized, civilized chic. The Art Deco lobby is decked out in huge mirrors and clever ceiling frescoes. There's also a stunning trompe l'oeil dining room. Guest rooms are testimonials to the sober Regency style, with weighty marble fireplaces and mahogany furnishings. ✉ *11 rue d'Astorg, 75008,* ☎ *01–53–05–05–05, 800/228–3000 in the U.S.,* FAX *01–53–05–05–30. 132 rooms and 3 suites. Restaurant, bar, air-conditioning, in-room modem lines, in-room safes, no-smoking rooms, room service, health club, laundry service. AE, DC, MC, V. Métro: Miromesnil, St-Augustin.*

$$$$ 🏨 **Le Bristol.** This hotel's understated facade might mislead the unknowing, but the Bristol ranks among Paris's top four hotels. Some of the spaciously elegant rooms have authentic Louis XV and Louis XVI furniture and magnificent marble bathrooms. The public areas are filled with Old Master paintings, sculptures, sumptuous carpets, and tapestries. Service throughout is impeccable. ✉ *112 rue du Faubourg St-Honoré, 75008,* ☎ *01–53–43–43–00,* FAX *01–53–43–43–01. 154 rooms and 41 suites. Restaurant, bar, air-conditioning, in-room safes, room service, indoor pool, sauna, health club, laundry service, meeting rooms, free parking. AE, DC, MC, V. Métro: St-Philippe-du-Roule.*

$$$$ 🏨 **Crillon.** The Crillon, comprising two 18th-century town houses on place de la Concorde, is often called the crème de la crème of Paris's "palace" hotels. Marie-Antoinette took singing lessons here; one of the original *grands appartements,* now protected as a national treasure, has been named after her. Rooms are lavishly decorated with Rococo and Directoire antiques, crystal and gilt wall sconces, and gold fittings. The sheer quantity of marble downstairs—especially in Les Ambassadeurs restaurant—is staggering. ⊠ *10 pl. de la Concorde, 75008,* ☎ *01–44–71–15–00,* FAX *01–44–71–15–02. 118 rooms and 45 suites. 2 restaurants, 2 bars, tea shop, air-conditioning, in-room safes, no-smoking rooms, room service, exercise room, meeting rooms. AE, DC, MC, V. Métro: Concorde.*

$$$$ 🏨 **Lancaster.** The Lancaster—one of Paris's most ven-
★ erable institutions—has been meticulously transformed into one of the city's most modish luxury hotels. The new decor seamlessly blends the traditional with the contemporary, from the hotel's specially commissioned line of scented bath products to the exquisite Porthault linens. Many of the suites pay homage to the hotel's colorful regulars from Garbo to Huston to Sir Alec Guinness. ⊠ *7 rue de Berri, 75008,* ☎ *01–40–76–40–76, 800/447–7462 in the U.S.,* FAX *01–40–76–40–00. 60 rooms and 8 suites. Restaurant, bar, air-conditioning, in-room safes, room service, in-room VCRs, sauna, exercise room, baby-sitting, laundry service, meeting rooms. AE, DC, MC, V. Métro: George-V.*

$$$$ 🏨 **Plaza-Athénée.** The Plaza, with its distinctive turn-of-the-century facade, is tucked discreetly among the haute couture houses on avenue Montaigne, just a block from the Champs-Elysées. Rooms, overlooking either the courtyard or the tony, tree-lined avenue, are superb examples of the Louis XV, Louis XVI, or Regency styles. The brand new fitness club affords views of the Eiffel Tower. ⊠ *25 av. Montaigne, 75008,* ☎ *01–53–67–66–65, 800/223–6800 in the U.S.,* FAX *01–53–67–66–66. 205 rooms and 65 suites. 2 restaurants, bar, air-conditioning, in-room modem lines, in-room safes, no-smoking rooms, room service, beauty salon, health club, laundry service, meeting rooms. AE, DC, MC, V. Métro: Alma-Marceau.*

$$ 🏨 **Résidence Monceau.** In one of the most privileged neighborhoods of Paris, this friendly, fashionable hotel is a calm oasis. Rooms are cozily draped in warm tones and the breakfast garden, surrounded by ivy-covered trellises, makes a lovely place to start the day. ⊠ *85 rue du Rocher, 75008,* ☎ *01–45–22–75–11,* FAX *01–45–22–*

30–88. 45 rooms with bath, 6 with shower. Bar, café, no-smoking rooms, travel services. AE, DC, MC, V. Métro: Villiers.

9° Arrondissement (Opéra)

$$$$ ⊞ **Grand Hôtel Inter-Continental.** Open since 1862, Paris's biggest luxury hotel has a facade that seems as long as the Louvre. The grand salon's Art Deco dome and the restaurant's painted ceilings are registered landmarks. The Art Deco rooms are spacious and light. ⊠ 2 rue Scribe, 75009, ☎ 01–40–07–32–32, 800/327–0200 in the U.S., ⅁ 01–42–66–12–51. 514 rooms and 39 suites. 3 restaurants, 2 bars, air-conditioning, in-room safes, no-smoking rooms, room service, in-room VCRs, sauna, health club, laundry service, meeting rooms. AE, DC, MC, V. Métro: Opéra.

12° Arrondissement (Bastille/Gare de Lyon)

$$ ⊞ **Le Pavillon Bastille.** The transformation of this 19th-
★ century hôtel particulier into a mod, colorful, high-design hotel garnered architectural awards and a devoted clientele. The gracious staff pours on the romantic extras (4 PM checkout, fluffy Porthault towels) and every detail is pitch perfect, right down to the 17th-century fountain in the garden. ⊠ 65 rue de Lyon, 75012, ☎ 01–43–43–65–65, 800/233–2552 in the U.S., ⅁ 01–43–43–96–52. 24 rooms and 1 suite. Bar, air-conditioning, in-room safes, minibars, room service. AE, DC, MC, V. Métro: Bastille.

14° Arrondissement (Montparnasse)

$$ ⊞ **Raspail-Montparnasse.** Rooms in this three-star hotel are named after the artists who made Montparnasse the art capital of the world in the '20s and '30s. All are decorated in pastel colors; five offer spectacular panoramic views of Montparnasse and the Eiffel Tower. Most rooms are at the low end of this price category. ⊠ 203 bd. Raspail, 75014, ☎ 01–43–20–62–86, ⅁ 01–43–20–50–79. 28 rooms with bath, 10 with shower. Bar,

*air-conditioning, in-room safes, meeting rooms. AE,
DC, MC, V. Métro: Vavin.*

$ ⊞ **Istria.** This small, charming family-run hotel on a quiet
side street was once a Montparnasse artists' hangout.
It has a flower-filled courtyard and simple, clean, comfortable rooms with soft pastel-toned Japanese wallpa-
per. ⊠ *29 rue Campagne-Première, 75014,* ☎
01–43–20–91–82, FAX *01–43–22–48–45. 4 rooms
with bath, 22 with shower. In-room safes, meeting
rooms. AE, DC, MC, V. Métro: Raspail.*

$ ⊞ **Parc Montsouris.** This modest two-star hotel in a
1930s villa on a quiet residential street next to the lovely
Parc Montsouris gets better every year. Rooms tend to
be small, but clean, tastefully furnished, and equipped
with satellite TV. Those with showers are very inexpensive. Suites sleep four. ⊠ *4 rue du Parc-Montsouris,
75014,* ☎ *01–45–89–09–72,* FAX *01–45–80–92–72.
28 rooms with bath, 7 suites with shower. AE, MC, V.
Métro: Montparnasse-Bienvenue.*

16ᵉ Arrondissement
(Trocadéro/Bois de Boulogne)

$$$$ ⊞ **Saint James Paris.** Called the "only château-hôtel in
★   Paris," this gracious late-19th-century neoclassical mansion is surrounded by a lush private park. The lavish Art
Deco interior was created by jet-set designer André Put-
nam. Ten rooms on the third floor open onto a winter
garden. The magnificent bar-library is lined with floor-
to-ceiling oak bookcases. The restaurant is reserved for
guests; in warm weather, meals are served in the garden. The poshest option: booking one of the two du-
plex gatehouses. ⊠ *43 av. Bugeaud, 75116,* ☎
01–44–05–81–81, FAX *01–44–05–81–82. 24 rooms
and 24 suites. Restaurant, bar, air-conditioning, in-
room safes, room service, sauna, health club, baby-sitting, laundry service, meeting rooms, free parking. AE,
DC, MC, V. Métro: Porte Dauphine.*

$–$$ ⊞ **Queen's Hotel.** One of only a handful of hotels in the
tony residential district near the Bois de Boulogne,
Queen's is a small, comfortable hotel. Each room focuses
on a different 20th-century French artist. The rooms with

baths have Jacuzzis. ⊠ *4 rue Bastien-Lepage, 75016,*
☎ *01–42–88–89–85,* ℻ *01–40–50–67–52. 7 rooms
with bath, 16 with shower. Air-conditioning, in-room
safes, no-smoking rooms. AE, DC, MC, V. Métro:
Michelange-Auteuil.*

17ᵉ Arrondissement (Monceau/Clichy)

$$
★ 🏨 **Etoile-Péreire.** This unique, intimate hotel consists of
two parts: a fin-de-siècle building on the street and a
1920s annex overlooking an interior courtyard. Rooms
and duplexes are decorated in deep shades of roses or
blues with crisp, white damask upholstery. The copious
breakfast is legendary, featuring 40 assorted jams and
jellies. ⊠ *146 bd. Péreire, 75017,* ☎ *01–42–67–60–
00,* ℻ *01–42–67–02–90. 18 rooms and 5 duplex
suites with bath, 3 rooms with shower. Bar, air-condi-
tioning in some rooms, no-smoking rooms, laundry ser-
vice. AE, DC, MC, V. Métro: Péreire.*

$$ 🏨 **Regent's Garden.** Built in the mid-19th century by
Napoléon III for his doctor, this hotel is adorned as you
would imagine with marble fireplaces, mirrors, gilt furniture, and cornicing. Be sure to request a room overlooking the gorgeous garden, where breakfast is served
in summer. ⊠ *6 rue Pierre-Demours, 75017,* ☎ *01–45–
74–07–30,* ℻ *01–40–55–01–42. 39 rooms. Lobby
lounge, air-conditioning in some rooms. AE, DC, MC,
V. Métro: Ternes.*

18ᵉ Arrondissement (Montmartre)

$ 🏨 **Ermitage.** This elfin, family-run hotel dates from
Napoléon III and is filled with antiques. The building
has only two stories, but the hilly Montmartre neighborhood ensures that some rooms have a nice view of
Paris. ⊠ *24 rue Lamarck, 75018,* ☎ *01–42–64–79–
22,* ℻ *01–42–64–10–33. 3 rooms with bath, 9 with
shower. No credit cards. Métro: Lamarck-Caulaincourt.*

$ 🏨 **Regyn's Montmartre.** Despite the small rooms, this
owner-run hotel on Montmartre's evocative place des
Abbesses provides comfortable accommodations. Each
floor is dedicated to a Montmartre artist; poetic homages

by local writers feature in the hallways. Ask for a room on either of the top two floors for great views of either the Eiffel Tower or Sacré-Coeur. ⊠ *18 pl. des Abbesses, 75018,* ☎ *01–42–54–45–21,* ℻ *01–42–23–76–69. 14 rooms with bath, 8 with shower. In-room safes. AE, MC, V. Métro: Abbesses.*

5 Nightlife and the Arts

THE ARTS

Updated
by Roberta
Beardsley

PARISIANS CONSIDER THEIR CITY a bastion of art and culture, and indeed it is. Enormous amounts of government money go into culture, but surprisingly, Paris is not quite on par with New York, London, or Milan for theater, opera, music, or ballet. Nonetheless, Parisian audiences are discerning, so standards are very high. Also, many international companies that you might not see elsewhere perform in Paris.

The music season usually runs from September to June. Theaters also stay open at this time, but many productions are at summer festivals elsewhere in France. The weekly magazines *Pariscope* (which has an English section), *L'Officiel des Spectacles,* and *Figaroscope* (a supplement to *Le Figaro* newspaper) are published every Wednesday and give detailed entertainment listings. The Paris Tourist Office's **24-hour hot line** in English (☎ 01–49–52–53–56) is another source of information about weekly events.

The best place to buy tickets is at the venue itself; try to purchase in advance, as many of the more popular performances sell out. Also try your hotel or a travel agency, such as **Paris-Vision** (⌧ 1 rue Auber, 9ᵉ, ☎ 01–40–06–01–00, métro Opéra). Tickets for some events can be bought at the **FNAC** stores—especially Alpha-FNAC (⌧ 1–5 rue Pierre Lescot, Forum des Halles, 3rd level down, 1ᵉʳ, ☎ 01–40–41–40–00, métro Châtelet-Les Halles). **Virgin Megastore** (⌧ 52 av. des Champs-Elysées, 8ᵉ, ☎ 01–44–78–44–08, métro Franklin-D.-Roosevelt) sells theater and concert tickets. Half-price tickets for many same-day theater performances are available at the **Kiosque Théâtre** (⌧ across from 15 pl. de la Madeleine, métro Madeleine), open Tuesday–Saturday, 12:30–8 and Sunday 12:30–6; expect a line. There's another branch inside the Châtelet RER station, open Monday–Saturday.

Classical Music

A varied program of classical and world music concerts are held at the new **Cité de la Musique** (⊠ 221 av. Jean-Jaurès, 19e, ☎ 01–44–84–44–84, métro Porte de Pantin). The **Salle Pleyel** (⊠ 252 rue du Faubourg-St-Honoré, 8e, ☎ 01–45–61–53–00, métro Ternes), was Paris's principal home of classical music before the new Opéra de la Bastille opened; the Paris Symphony Orchestra and other leading international orchestras still play here regularly. The **Théâtre des Champs-Elysées** (⊠ 15 av. Montaigne, 8e, ☎ 01–49–52–50–50, métro Alma-Marceau), an Art Deco temple, hosts concerts and ballet as well as plays.

Paris also has a never-ending stream of free or inexpensive lunchtime and evening church concerts, ranging from organ recitals to choral music and orchestral works. Some are scheduled as part of the **Festival d'Art Sacré** (☎ 01–44–70–64–10, for information) between mid-November and Christmas. Check the weekly listings for information; telephone numbers for most church concerts vary with the organizer. **Ste-Chapelle** (⊠ 4 bd. du Palais, 1er, métro Cité) holds outstanding candlelit concerts, though not in winter; make reservations well in advance. Other churches holding classical concerts—ranging from organ recitals to choral music and orchestral works—include (☞ Chapter 2 for addresses): **Notre-Dame, St-Germain-des-Prés,** and **St-Louis-en-l'Ile.**

Dance

Opéra Garnier (⊠ pl. de l'Opéra, 9e, ☎ 01–40–01–17–89, métro Opéra) is the sumptuous home of the well-reputed Paris Ballet, as well as host to many major foreign dance troupes. **Théâtre de la Bastille** (⊠ 76 rue de la Roquette, ☎ 01–43–57–42–14, 11e, métro Bastille) merits mention as an example of the innovative activity in the Bastille area; it has an enviable record as a launch pad for tomorrow's modern dance stars. **Théâtre de la Ville** (⊠ 2 pl. du Châtelet, 4e, métro Châtelet and ⊠ 31 rue des Abbesses, 18e, métro Abbesses, ☎ 01–42–74–22–77 for both) has a varied international dance program.

Film

Parisians are far more addicted to film as an art form than Londoners or New Yorkers. A number of theaters, especially in principal tourist areas such as the Champs-Elysées, the boulevard des Italiens near the Opéra, St-Germain-des-Prés, and Les Halles, run English-language films. Check the weekly guides for a movie of your choice with the initials "v.o." or "v.o.s.t.f.," which means *version original/sous titrés français,* or not dubbed. Showings of classic and independent films are common, especially in the Latin Quarter (check "Festivals" in weekly guides). Cinema admission runs from 37 to 51 francs.

Big-screen fanatics should try the **Grand Rex** (⊠ 1 bd. Poissonière, 2ᵉ, ☎ 08–36–68–70–23, métro Bonne Nouvelle). The **Max Linder Panorama** (⊠ 24 bd. Poissonière, 9ᵉ, ☎ 01–48–24–88–88, métro Rue Montmartre) often shows classics on its big screen. The Chinese-style **La Pagode** (⊠ 57 bis rue de Babylone, 7ᵉ, ☎ 01–45–55–48–48, métro François-Xavier) is a national monument and well worth a visit.

Opera

Opéra de la Bastille (⊠ pl. de la Bastille, 11ᵉ, ☎ 01–47–73–13–00, métro Bastille) has taken over the role as Paris's main opera house from the Opéra Garnier, but many feel it is not living up to its promise of grand opera at affordable prices (which range from 60 to 590 francs). **Opéra Garnier** (⊠ pl. de l'Opéra, 9ᵉ, ☎ 01–40–01–17–89, métro Opéra) still hosts occasional performances of the Paris Opéra. **Théâtre Musical de Paris** (⊠ pl. du Châtelet, 1ᵉʳ, ☎ 01–40–28–28–28, métro Châtelet), better known as the Théâtre du Châtelet, offers opera and ballet for a wider audience than the Opéra Garnier, at more reasonable prices.

Puppet Shows

On most Wednesday, Saturday, and Sunday afternoons, the Guignol, the French equivalent of Punch and Judy, can be seen going through their ritualistic battles in a number of Paris's parks, including: **Champs de Mars** (métro Ecole Militaire) and **Parc Montsouris** (métro Porte d'Orléans); and the **Jardin du Luxembourg** (métro Vavin) and the **Jardin d'Ac-climatation** (métro Sablons), both of which have year-round, weather-proof spaces.

Theater

A number of theaters line the Grand Boulevards between Opéra and République, but there is no Paris equivalent to Broadway or the West End. Shows are mostly in French. A fun spot to experience a particularly Parisian form of theater, the *café-théâtre*—a mixture of satirical sketches and variety show riddled with slapstick humor and viewed in a café setting—is at the **Café de la Gare** (⊠ 41 rue du Temple, 4ᵉ, ☎ 01–42–78–52–51, métro Rambuteau). You need a good grasp of French. **Comédie Française** (⊠ pl. André-Malraux, 1ᵉʳ, ☎ 01–44–58–15–15, métro Palais-Royal) is a distinguished venue that stages classical drama. **Théâtre de la Huchette** (⊠ 23 rue de la Huchette, 5ᵉ, ☎ 01–43–26–38–99, métro St-Michel) is a highlight for Ionesco admirers; this tiny Left Bank theater is where the playwright's short modern plays make a deliberate mess of the French language. **Théâtre de l'Odéon** (⊠ pl. de l'Odéon, 6ᵉ, ☎ 01–44–41–36–36, métro Odéon) hosts first-rate companies from all over Europe; subtitles (in French) are part of the program.

NIGHTLIFE

So you've immersed yourself in culture all day and you want a night out on the town. The hottest spots are around Pigalle—despite its reputation as a seedy red-light district—and the Bastille and Marais areas. The Left Bank has a bit of everything. The Champs-Elysées is making a comeback, though the clientele remains predominantly foreign. On week nights, people are usually home after closing hours at 2 AM, but weekends mean late-night partying. Take note, though: The last métro runs between 12:30 and 1 AM (but you can always take a cab).

Bars de Nuit

Buddha Bar (⊠ 8 rue Boissy d'Anglas, 8ᵉ, ☎ 01–53–05–90–00, métro Concorde), with its imposing Buddha contemplating the fashionable crowd, has a spacious mezzanine bar that overlooks the dining room where cuisines, east and west, meet somewhere in California.

Le Closerie des Lilas (⊠ 171 bd. de Montparnasse, 6ᵉ, ☎ 01–43–54–21–68, RER Port Royal) has served more than one generation of poets and intellectuals, as the brass plaques around the bar attest. The piano plays until one in the morning.

Le Forum (⊠ 4 bd. Malesherbes, 8ᵉ, ☎ 01–42–65–37–86, métro Madeleine), a discreet, archetypal French cocktail bar, has one of the best selections of cocktails and whiskeys in Paris.

Harry's New York Bar (⊠ 5 rue Daunou, 2ᵉ, ☎ 01–42–61–71–14, métro Opéra), a cozy, wood-paneled hangout popular with expatriates, is haunted by the ghosts of Ernest Hemingway and F. Scott Fitzgerald.

Moloko (⊠ 26 rue Fontaine, 9ᵉ, ☎ 01–48–74–50–26, métro Blanche), a smoky late-night bar with several rooms, a mezzanine, a jukebox, and a small dance floor, is a popular spot.

Boîtes de Nuit

Paris's *boîtes de nuit* (nightclubs) are both expensive and exclusive—it's best to know someone to get through the door. But the less affluent '90s have been a humbling experience for more than a few. Given the fragility of a club's life, it's best to check before going out. Many clubs are closed Monday and some on Tuesday; by Wednesday most are functioning at full swing.

Les Bains (⊠ 7 rue du Bourg-l'Abbé, 3ᵉ, ☎ 01–48–87–01–80, métro Etienne-Marcel), a forever-trendy hot spot with controversial new decor, combines bar, restaurant, and club, and is hard to get into. It's open every day of the week.

Chez Félix (⊠ 23 rue Mouffetard, 5ᵉ, ☎ 01–47–07–68–78, métro Monge) pulls in aficionados of live Brazilian music on Saturday nights. Their formula is a prix-fixe dinner with the show and dancing afterwards.

Le Colonial (⊠ moored at Port Debilly opposite the Eiffel Tower, 16ᵉ, ☎ 01–53–23–98–98, métro Pont de l'Alma) offers a port in the storm for those looking for an alterna-

Pick up
the phone.

Pick up
the miles.

Calling Card

415 555 1234 2244
J.D. SMITH

WorldPhone

Use your MCI Card® to make an international call from virtually anywhere in the world and earn frequent flyer miles on one of seven major airlines.

Enroll in an MCI Airline Partner Program today. In the U.S., call **1-800-FLY-FREE.** Overseas, call MCI collect at **1-916-567-5151.**

1. To use your MCI Card, just dial the WorldPhone access number of the country you're calling from.
   (For a complete listing of codes, visit www.mci.com.)
2. Dial or give the operator your MCI Card number.
3. Dial or give the number you're calling.

# Austria (CC) ♦	022-903-012
# Belarus (CC)	
From Brest, Vitebsk, Grodno, Minsk	8-800-103
From Gomel and Mogilev regions	8-10-800-103
# Belgium (CC) ♦	0800-10012
# Bulgaria	00800-0001
# Croatia (CC) ★	99-385-0112
# Czech Republic (CC) ♦	00-42-000112
# Denmark (CC) ♦	8001-0022
# Finland (CC) ♦	08001-102-80
# France (CC) ♦	0-800-99-0019
# Germany (CC)	0130-0012
# Greece (CC) ♦	00-800-1211
# Hungary (CC) ♦	00▼800-01411
# Iceland (CC) ♦	800-9002
# Ireland (CC)	1-800-55-1001
# Italy (CC) ♦	172-1022
# Kazakhstan (CC)	8-800-131-4321
# Liechtenstein (CC) ♦	0800-89-0222
# Luxembourg	0800-0112
# Monaco (CC) ♦	800-90-019

# Netherlands (CC) ♦	0800-022-91-22
# Norway (CC) ♦	800-19912
# Poland (CC) ÷	00-800-111-21-22
# Portugal (CC) ÷	05-017-1234
Romania (CC) ÷	01-800-1800
# Russia (CC) ÷ ♦	
To call using ROSTELCOM ■	747-3322
For a Russian-speaking operator	747-3320
To call using SOVINTEL ■	960-2222
# San Marino (CC) ♦	172-1022
# Slovak Republic (CC)	00-421-00112
# Slovenia	080-8808
# Spain (CC)	900-99-0014
# Sweden (CC) ♦	020-795-922
# Switzerland (CC) ♦	0800-89-0222
# Turkey (CC) ♦	00-8001-1177
# Ukraine (CC) ÷	.8▼10-013
# United Kingdom (CC)	
To call using BT ■	0800-89-0222
To call using MERCURY ■	0500-89-0222
# Vatican City (CC)	172-1022

Is this a great time, or what? :-)

Urban planning.

CITYPACKS

The ultimate guide to the city—a complete pocket guide plus a full-size color map.

tive to the Pigalle scene. The sizable disco has replaced the first-class cabins.

Keur Samba (✉ 79 rue La Boétie, 8ᵉ, ☎ 01–43–59–03–10, métro St-Philippe-du-Roule) has African decor and rhythms, a tiny dance floor, and an exclusive clientele who stays until dawn.

Cabarets

Paris's cabarets are household names, shunned by worldly Parisians and loved by tourists, who flock to the shows. You can dine at many of them: prices range from 200 francs (simple admission plus one drink) to more than 750 francs (dinner plus show). For 400 to 500 francs, you get a seat plus half a bottle of champagne.

Au Lapin Agile (✉ 22 rue des Saules, 18ᵉ, ☎ 01–46–06–85–87, métro Lamarck-Caulaincourt), in Montmartre, considers itself the doyen of cabarets. Picasso once paid for a meal with one of his paintings. Prices are lower than elsewhere, as this is more of a large bar than a full-blown cabaret.

Crazy Horse (✉ 12 av. George V, 8ᵉ, ☎ 01–47–23–32–32, métro Alma-Marceau) is one of the best-known clubs for pretty girls and raunchy dance routines with lots of humor and few clothes.

Folies Bergère (✉ 32 rue Richer, 9ᵉ, ☎ 01–44–79–98–98, métro Cadet), a legend since the days of Manet, is now a new-and-improved cabaret that returns to its music-hall origins, helped by ornate costumes and masterful lighting.

Lido (✉ 116 bis av. des Champs-Elysées, 8ᵉ, ☎ 01–40–76–56–10, métro George V) stars the famous Bluebell Girls; the owners claim no show this side of Las Vegas can rival it for special effects.

Moulin Rouge (✉ 82 bd. de Clichy, 18ᵉ, ☎ 01–46–06–00–19, métro Blanche), that old favorite at the foot of Montmartre, mingles the Doriss girls, the cancan, and crocodiles in an extravagant spectacle.

Gay and Lesbian Bars and Clubs

Gay and lesbian bars and clubs are mostly concentrated in the Marais and include some of the hippest addresses in the city. However, trendy clubs fall in and out of favor at lightning speed, and one-night discos and tea dances are always popping up, so check the local papers to see what's hot.

Amnésia Café (⊠ 42 rue Vieille-du-Temple, 4ᵉ, ☎ 01–42–72–16–94, métro Rambuteau) has an underlit bar and art deco ceiling paintings that attract a young, yuppie gay and lesbian crowd.

Champmesle (⊠ 4 rue Chabanais, 2ᵉ, ☎ 01–42–96–85–20, métro Bourse) is the hub of lesbian nightlife, with a dusky back room reserved for women only.

Queen (⊠ 102 av. des Champs-Elysées, 8ᵉ, ☎ 01–53–89–08–90, métro George V) is currently one of the most talked about nightclubs in Paris: Gays, lesbians, and heterosexuals are all lining up to get in. Monday is disco night, with house music on other days.

Jazz Clubs

The French take jazz seriously, and Paris is one of the world's great jazz cities, with plenty of variety, including some fine, distinctive local talent. Most jazz clubs are in the Latin Quarter or around Les Halles. For nightly schedules, consult the specialty magazine *Jazz Hot* or *Jazz Magazine*. Remember that nothing gets going until 10 or 11 PM and that entry prices vary widely from about 40 francs to more than 100 francs.

Caveau de la Huchette (⊠ 5 rue de la Huchette, 5ᵉ, ☎ 01–43–26–65–05, métro St-Michel) is a smoke-filled shrine to the Dixieland beat.

Le Petit Journal (⊠ 71 bd. St-Michel, 5ᵉ, ☎ 01–43–26–28–59, RER Luxembourg) has long attracted leading exponents of New Orleans jazz; it serves good food, too.

New Morning (⊠ 7 rue des Petites-Ecuries, 10ᵉ, ☎ 01–45–23–51–41, métro Château-d'Eau) is a premier spot for serious fans of avant-garde jazz, folk, and world music; decor is spartan, the mood reverential.

Rock, Pop, and World Music Venues

Unlike French jazz, French rock is not generally considered to be on a par with its American and British cousins. Even so, Paris is a great place to catch some of your favorite groups because concert halls tend to be smaller and tickets can be less expensive. It's also a good spot to see all kinds of world music. Most places charge from 90 to 120 francs for entrance and get going around 11 PM.

Le Bataclan (⊠ 50 bd. Voltaire, 11ᵉ, ☎ 01–47–00–30–12, métro Oberkampf) is a legendary venue for live rock, rap, and reggae in an intimate setting with a disco that gets going after-hours.

Casino de Paris (⊠ 16 rue de Clichy, 9ᵉ, ☎ 01–49–95–99–99, métro Trinité), once a favorite with Serge Gainsbourg, has a horseshoe balcony and a cramped, cozy, music-hall feel.

Divan du Monde (⊠ 75 rue des Martyrs, 18ᵉ, ☎ 01–44–92–77–66, métro Pigalle) is on every music fan's list. The crowd varies according to the music of the evening: reggae, soul, funk, or salsa.

Elysée Montmartre (⊠ 72 bd. Rochechouart, 18ᵉ, ☎ 01–44–92–45–45, métro Anvers) dates from Gustave Eiffel, its builder, who, it's hoped, liked a good party. With a following as diverse as the music, and a new techno sound system, it provides a new definition of the old *bal populaire*.

Wine Bars

Paris wine bars are the perfect place to enjoy a glass (or bottle) of wine with a plate of cheese or charcuterie. Bar owners are often true wine enthusiasts ready to dispense expert advice. Hours can vary widely, so it's best to check ahead if your heart is set on a particular place; most, however, close around 10 PM.

Le Baron Rouge (⊠ 1 rue Théophile-Roussel, 12ᵉ, ☎ 01–43–43–14–32, métro Ledru-Rollin) is a dark, noisy haunt, where wine spills from the barrel. It's every bit as rambunctious as the nearby place d'Aligre (famous for its market).

La Robe et le Palais (⊠ 13 rue des Lavandières-Ste-Opportune, 1ᵉʳ, ☎ 01–45–08–07–41, métro Châtelet) offers over 120 wines from all over France, served *au compteur* (according to the quantity consumed).

6 Shopping

Updated
by
Suzanne
Rowan
Kelleher

W

INDOW-SHOPPING is one of Paris's greatest spectator sports. Tastefully displayed wares—luscious cream-filled éclairs, lacy lingerie, exquisite clothing, and gleaming copper pots—entice the eye and awaken the imagination. Happily, shopping opportunities in Paris are endless. For many, perfume and designer clothing are perhaps the most coveted Parisian souvenirs. However, even on haute couture's home turf, bargains are surprisingly elusive. It's best to know prices before coming, to avoid the slings and arrows of international exchange rates. A Lalique bottle of L'Air du Temps may be cheaper at the mall back home, although it won't be as much fun to buy.

Bargain hunters should watch for the word *soldes* (sales). The two main sale seasons are January and July. Credit cards are more widely used in France than in the United States. Even the corner newsstand or flea market are likely to honor plastic for purchases over 100 francs. Visa is the most common and preferred card, followed closely by Master-Card/EuroCard. American Express, Diners Club, and Access are accepted in the larger international stores.

Duty-Free Shopping

A value-added tax of 20.6%, known in France as the TVA or *détaxe,* is imposed on most consumer goods. Non–European Union residents, aged 15 and over, who stay in France and/or the EU for fewer than six months can reclaim part of this tax. To qualify, your purchases in a single shop must total at least 1,200 francs. The amount of the refund varies from shop to shop but usually hovers between 13% and 16%. You may opt to be reimbursed by check, but a refund credited directly to your credit card is the easiest and fastest way to receive your money. The major department stores have simplified the process with special détaxe desks where the *bordereaux* (export sales invoices) are prepared. Most high-profile shops with international clients have détaxe forms, but stores are not required to do this paperwork. If the discount is extremely important to you, ask if it is available before making your purchase. There is no refund for food, wine, and tobacco. Invoices and bordereaux forms must be presented to French customs upon leaving the country. The items purchased should be available for inspection.

Shopping Areas

Avenue Montaigne

This exclusive, elegant boulevard is a showcase of international haute-couture houses. Italian moguls Prada and Dolce & Gabbana have joined Chanel, Dior, Nina Ricci, Guy Laroche, Emanuel Ungaro, Céline, Valentino, and the like. Here you'll also find accessories by S. T. Dupont, Loewe, Salvatore Ferragamo, and Louis Vuitton. Yves Saint-Laurent and Givenchy are nearby, on avenues Marceau and George-V, respectively, and you'll find Versace on rue François I.

Bastille

Scores of trendy boutiques are clustered between art galleries, bars, and furniture stores in this gentrified neighborhood. Jean-Paul Gaultier has a boutique on rue Faubourg St-Antoine and hot, young newcomer Christophe Lemaire is installed on the rue St-Sabin.

Champs-Elysées

Cafés and movie theaters keep the once chic Champs-Elysées active 24 hours a day, but the invasion of exchange banks, car showrooms, and fast-food chains has lowered the tone. Four glitzy 20th-century arcade malls (Galerie du Lido, Le Rond-Point, Le Claridge, and Elysées 26) capture most of the retail action.

Left Bank

After decades of clustering on the Right Bank's venerable shopping avenues, the high-fashion houses are now storming the Rive Gauche. Ever since Louis Vuitton, Giorgio Armani, Thierry Mugler, Christian Dior Men, and Romeo Gigli set up Left Bank shops in 1996, anyone who's anyone has rushed to followed suit. This immensely walkable district between rue de Grenelle and rue de Rennes is also known for its top-quality shoe shops (Maud Frizon, Charles Jourdan, Stephane Kélian, and Harel).

Les Halles

Most of the narrow pedestrian streets on the former site of Paris's wholesale food market are lined with fast-food joints, sex shops, jeans outlets, and garish souvenir stands, but rue du Jour (featuring MaxMara, agnès b., and Junior Gaultier boutiques) is an attractive exception. The fabulously quirky Comme des Garçons has shops for both sexes on rue Etienne-Marcel. In the middle of the action is the Forum des Halles, a multilevel underground shopping mall, which used to be a nightmarish mash of noisy teens until it attracted higher-quality merchants and a clutch of promising designers.

Louvre–Palais-Royal

The elegant and eclectic shops clustered in the 18th-century arcades of the Palais-Royal sell antiques, toy soldiers, Shiseido cosmetics, dramatic art jewelry from Siki, and even vintage designer dresses. The glossy marble Carrousel du Louvre mall, beneath the Louvre, is lit by an immense inverted glass pyramid. Shops, including Virgin Megastore, the Body Shop, and Esprit, along with a lively international food court, are open on Sunday—still a rare convenience in Paris.

Le Marais

Between the pre-Revolution mansions and tiny kosher food stores that characterize this area are scores of trendy gift shops and clothing stores. Avant-garde designers Azzedine Alaïa, Lolita Lempicka, Issey Miyake, and Romeo Gigli have boutiques within a few blocks of the stately place des Vosges and the Picasso and Carnavalet museums. A growing number of Marais shops are open on Sunday afternoons.

Montparnasse

Montparnasse is better known for bars and restaurants than shops. Rue d'Alésia on the southern fringe of Montparnasse is known for discount clothing shops.

Opéra to Madeleine

Three major department stores—Au Printemps, Galeries Lafayette, and the British Marks & Spencer—define boulevard Haussmann, behind Paris's ornate 19th-century Opéra Garnier. Place de la Madeleine is home to two luxurious food stores, Fauchon and Hédiard. Lalique and Baccarat

Crystal also have opulent showrooms near the Eglise de la Madeleine.

Place Vendôme and Rue de la Paix

The magnificent 17th-century place Vendôme, home of the Ritz Hotel, and rue de la Paix, leading north from Vendôme, have attracted the world's most elegant jewelers: Cartier, Boucheron, Buccellati, Van Cleef and Arpels, Répossi, Mellerio, Mauboussin, and Mikimoto.

Place des Victoires

This graceful, circular plaza near the Palais-Royal is the playground of cutting-edge fashion icons such as Kenzo, Victoire, and Thierry Mugler. Avant-garde boutiques like Chantal Thomass, Jean-Charles de Castelbajac, Absinthe, and En Attendant les Barbares have fanned into the side streets; Jean-Paul Gaultier's flagship shop is in the nearby Galerie Vivienne arcade. One of the hottest new emporiums to pop up in the neighborhood, Le Shop, at 3 rue d'Argout, rents retail space to hip, up-and-coming designers.

Rue du Faubourg St-Honoré

The Paris branch of Sotheby's and renowned antiques galleries such as Didier Aaron add artistic flavor to the grand presence of the Elysée Palace. Boutiques include Hermès, Lanvin, Karl Lagerfeld, Reveillon Furs, Louis Feraud, and Christian Lacroix.

Department Stores

Paris's top department stores are mostly open Monday through Saturday from about 9:30 AM to 7 PM, and some are open until 10 PM one weekday evening. All major stores listed below have multilingual guides, international welcome desks, détaxe offices, and restaurants. Most are on the Right Bank, near the Opéra and the Hôtel de Ville; the notable exception is Au Bon Marché on the Left Bank.

Au Bon Marché (⊠ 22 rue de Sèvres, 7ᵉ, ☎ 01–44–39–80–00, métro Sèvres-Babylone), founded in 1852, is an excellent hunting ground for linens, table settings, and high-quality furniture on the Left Bank. The new ground-floor Balthazar men's shop feels like a smart boutique. La

Grande Epicerie, one of the largest groceries in Paris is a gourmet's mecca.

Au Printemps (⊠ 64 bd. Haussmann, 9ᵉ, ☎ 01–42–82–50–00, métro Havre-Caumartin, Opéra, or Auber) has three newly revamped floors of women's fashion featuring hot designers like Helmut Lang, Dolce & Gabbana, and the Spanish line, Zara. Free fashion shows are held on Tuesday (all year) and Friday (March–October) at 10 AM under the cupola on the 7th floor of La Mode, the building dedicated to women's and children's fashion. The three-store complex also includes La Maison, for housewares and furniture, and Brummel, a six-floor emporium devoted to menswear.

Galeries Lafayette (⊠ 40 bd. Haussmann, 9ᵉ, ☎ 01–42–82–34–56, métro Chaussée d'Antin, Opéra, or Havre-Caumartin; ⊠ Centre Commercial Montparnasse, 15ᵉ, ☎ 01–45–38–52–87, métro Montparnasse-Bienvenue) carries nearly 80,000 fashion labels under its roof, including rising stars like Mariot Chanet, Ann Demeulemeester, and Marcel Marongiou. Along with the world's largest perfumery, the main store boasts the new "Espace Lafayette Maison," a huge Yves Taralon–designed emporium dedicated to the art of living *à la française*.

Marks & Spencer (⊠ 35 bd. Haussmann, 9ᵉ, ☎ 01–47–42–42–91, métro Havre-Caumartin, Auber, or Opéra; ⊠ 88 rue de Rivoli, 4ᵉ, ☎ 01–44–61–08–00, métro Hôtel de Ville) is a British chain chiefly noted for its moderately priced basics (underwear, socks, sleep- and sportswear). Its excellent English grocery store and take-out food service are enormously popular with Parisians.

La Samaritaine (⊠ 19 rue de la Monnaie, 1ᵉʳ, ☎ 01–40–41–20–20, métro Pont-Neuf or Châtelet), a sprawling five-store complex, carries everything from designer fashions to cuckoo clocks but is especially known for kitchen supplies, housewares, and furniture. Its most famous asset is the rooftop café in Building 2 that offers a marvelous view of Notre-Dame.

Budget

Monoprix or Prisunic are French dime stores—with scores of branches throughout the city—that stock inexpensive everyday items like toothpaste, groceries, toys, typing paper, and bath mats—a little of everything. Most Parisians dash into their neighborhood stores at least once a week.

Specialty Shops

Art and Antiques

Art galleries and antiques shops are scattered throughout the city, though some that offer items from a specific period are clustered in certain neighborhoods. Many contemporary art galleries can be found around the Pompidou Center, the Picasso Museum, and the Bastille Opera. Often these galleries are in the courtyard of a building, the only sign of their presence a small plaque; take it as an invitation to push through the double doors. The carré Rive Gauche (métro St-Germain-des-Prés, Rue du Bac), an area that shelters dozens of art and antique galleries on its narrow lanes, is a good place to start. Works by old masters and established modern artists dominate the galleries around rue du Faubourg St-Honoré and avenue Matignon. To plot your course, get the free map published by the Association des Galeries; it's available at many galleries.

Louvre des Antiquaires (⊠ 2 pl. du Palais-Royal, 1er, métro Palais-Royal) is an elegant multifloor complex where 250 of Paris's leading dealers showcase their rarest objects, including Louis XV furniture, tapestries, and antique jewelry. The center is open Tuesday to Sunday; it's closed Sunday in July and August.

Bags, Scarves, and Accessories

Hermès (⊠ 24 rue du Faubourg St-Honoré, 8e, ☎ 01–40–17–47–17, métro Concorde) was established as a saddlery in 1837 and went on to create the famous, eternally chic Kelly bag for Grace Kelly. The magnificent silk scarves—truly fashion icons—are legendary for their rich colors and intricate designs, which change yearly. During biannual sales, in January and July, the astronomical prices are slashed by up to 50%.

Longchamp (⊠ 390 rue St-Honoré, 1er, ☎ 01–42–60–00–00, métro Concorde) sells bags and leather goods of excellent quality and impeccable taste. Its name has tremendous cachet with the famously brand-conscious Parisians.

Losco (✉ 20 rue de Sévigné, 4ᵉ, ☎ 01–48–04–39–93, métro St-Paul) allows customers to design their own high-quality belt by mixing and matching buckles and straps. There is a wide selection of styles and colors. Prices are reasonable.

Louis Vuitton (✉ 54 av. Montaigne, 8ᵉ, ☎ 01–45–62–90–43, métro Franklin-D.-Roosevelt; ✉ 78 av. Marceau, 8ᵉ, ☎ 01–47–20–47–00, métro George-V; ✉ 6 pl. St-Germain-des-Prés, 6ᵉ, ☎ 01–45–49–62–32, métro St-Germain-des-Prés) catapulted back to the fashion pinnacle by persuading designers like Helmut Lang, Vivienne Westwood, and Azzedine Alaïa to create a daring new series of bags with the famous monogrammed canvas. The results are anything but over-exposed.

Bookstores (English-Language)

The scenic open-air bookstalls along the Seine, selling secondhand books (mostly in French), prints, and souvenirs, are a major tourist attraction. Numerous French-language bookshops are found in the scholarly Latin Quarter and the publishing district, St-Germain-des-Prés.

Brentano's (✉ 37 av. de l'Opéra, 2ᵉ, ☎ 01–42–61–52–50, métro Opéra) is stocked with everything from classics to children's titles.

Shakespeare & Company (✉ 37 rue de la Bûcherie, 5ᵉ, no phone, métro St-Michel), the sentimental Left Bank favorite, specializes in expatriate literature.

W. H. Smith (✉ 248 rue de Rivoli, 1ᵉʳ, ☎ 01–44–78–88–89, métro Concorde) carries an excellent range of travel and language books, cookbooks, and fiction for adults and children.

Clothing (Women's)

CLASSIC CHIC

Chanel (✉ 42 av. Montaigne, 8ᵉ, ☎ 01–47–23–74–12, métro Franklin-D.-Roosevelt; ✉ 31 rue Cambon, 1ᵉʳ, ☎ 01–42–86–28–00, métro Tuileries), the most successful of all couture houses, is helmed by Karl Lagerfeld, a master at updating Coco's signature look with fresh colors and free-spirited silhouettes.

Christian Dior (✉ 30 av. Montaigne, 8ᵉ, ☎ 01–40–73–56–07, métro Franklin-D.-Roosevelt) installed the flamboyant

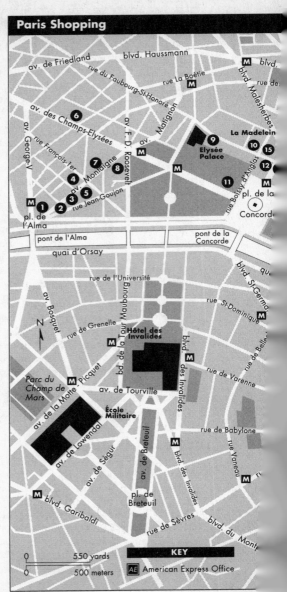

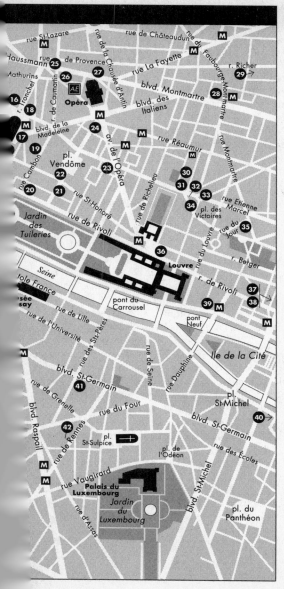

British designer, John Galliano, as head designer after his triumphant run at Givenchy. His wonderfully dramatic creations are sparkling homages to Dior's elegance.

Givenchy (✉ 3 av. George V, 8ᵉ, ☎ 01–44–31–50–00, métro Alma-Marceau) made headlines when it chose another bad boy Briton, Alexander McQueen, to take over where Galliano left off. Across the street at No. 8, Givenchy Boutique presents slightly more affordable versions of the designer's elegant ready-to-wear.

Nina Ricci (✉ 39 av. Montaigne, 8ᵉ, ☎ 01–49–52–56–00, métro Franklin-D.-Roosevelt) designs, with the trademark bow, are supremely ladylike; the lingerie is luxuriantly romantic. Ricci Club, for men, is next door.

TRENDSETTERS

Jean-Paul Gaultier (✉ 6 rue Vivienne, 2ᵉ, ☎ 01–42–86–05–05, métro Bourse or Palais-Royal), who made his name as Madonna's irreverent clothier, continues to create outrageously attention-getting garments for men and women.

Lolita Lempicka (✉ 13 bis rue Pavée, 4ᵉ, ☎ 01–42–74–50–48, métro St-Paul) serves up sharp suits and whimsical silk dresses. Studio Lolita, which sells last season's items at a discount, is across the street.

Thierry Mugler (✉ 45 rue du Bac, 6ᵉ, ☎ 01–45–44–44–44, métro Rue du Bac; ✉ 10 pl. des Victoires, 2ᵉ, ☎ 01–42–60–06–37, métro Bourse or Palais-Royal; ✉ 49 av. Montaigne, 8ᵉ, ☎ 01–47–23–37–62, métro Franklin-D.-Roosevelt) moved his empire to the Left Bank and brought his trademark curve-hugging shapes with him. His new Mugler Trade Mark line is a younger, funkier, and gentler-priced look.

Victoire (✉ 12 pl. des Victoires, 2ᵉ, ☎ 01–42–61–09–02, métro Bourse or Palais-Royal; menswear at ✉ 10–12 rue du Col. Driant, 1ᵉʳ, ☎ 01–42–97–44–87, métro Palais-Royal) is a discreet boutique with a knack for identifying new trends. What you buy here will be so far ahead of its time that you'll wear it for years. The Victoire menswear shop is a few steps away.

CHIC AND CASUAL

agnès b. (✉ 3, 6, and 10 rue du Jour, 1ᵉʳ, ☎ 01–45–08–56–56, métro Les Halles) makes knitwear separates in neutral colors that are wardrobe basics for young Parisians. Her various lines are sold as follows: children at No. 2, women at No. 3, men at No. 6, and the teenage line at No. 10.

Inès de la Fressange (⊠ 14 av. Montaigne, 8ᵉ, ☎ 01–47–23–08–94, métro Franklin-D.-Roosevelt; ⊠ 81 rue des St-Pères, 6ᵉ, ☎ 01–45–44–99–66, métro St-Germain-des-Prés), the former Chanel supermodel, recently expanded her empire of impeccably-tailored fashions to include colorful home decor.

Sonia Rykiel (⊠ 175 bd. St-Germain, 6ᵉ, ☎ 01–49–54–60–60, métro St-Germain-des-Prés; ⊠ 70 rue du Faubourg St-Honoré, 8ᵉ, ☎ 01–42–65–20–81, métro Concorde; ⊠ 64 rue d'Alésia, 14ᵉ, ☎ 01–43–95–06–13, métro Alésia) designs stylish, knitted separates and dresses for active women. The shop on rue d'Alésia sells last season's collection at a significant discount.

Clothing (Men's)

Charvet (⊠ 28 pl. Vendôme, 1ᵉʳ, ☎ 01–42–60–30–70, métro Opéra) is the Parisian equivalent of a Savile Row tailor: a conservative, aristocratic institution famed for made-to-measure shirts.

Façonnable (⊠ 9 rue du Faubourg St-Honoré, 8ᵉ, ☎ 01–47–42–72–60, métro Concorde) sells fashionable town and weekend clothes for young urbanites.

Food and Wine

Le Cave Augé (⊠ 116 bd. Haussmann, 8ᵉ, ☎ 01–45–22–16–97, métro St-Augustin), one of the best wine shops in Paris since 1850, is just the ticket whether you're looking for a rare vintage for a oenophile friend or a seductive Bordeaux for a tête-à-tête. English-speaking Marc Sibard is a knowledgeable and affable adviser.

Fauchon (⊠ 26 pl. de la Madeleine, 8ᵉ, ☎ 01–47–42–60–11, métro Madeleine), established in 1886, sells renowned pâté, honey, jelly, and private-label champagne. Hard-to-find foreign foods (U.S. pancake mix, British lemon curd) are also stocked.

Hédiard (⊠ 21 pl. de la Madeleine, 8ᵉ, ☎ 01–42–66–44–36, métro Madeleine), established in 1854, was famous in the 19th century for its imported spices. These—along with rare teas and beautifully packaged house brands of jam, mustard, and cookies—are still sold in this handsome shop.

Housewares

Baccarat Crystal (⊠ 30 bis rue de Paradis, 10ᵉ, ☎ 01–47–70–64–30, métro Château-d'Eau or Gare de l'Est) may not have many bargains, but this elegant, red-carpeted showroom with an in-house museum is worth a visit.

Christofle (⊠ 24 rue de la Paix, 2ᵉ, ☎ 01–42–65–62–43, métro Opéra; ⊠ 9 rue Royale, 8ᵉ, ☎ 01–49–33–43–00, métro Concorde or Madeleine), founded in 1830, is *the* name to know in French silver.

Lalique (⊠ 11 rue Royale, 8ᵉ, ☎ 01–42–66–52–40, métro Madeleine) crystal vases and statuettes are prized for their sinuous, romantic forms and delicate design.

La Vaissellerie (⊠ 80 bd. Haussmann, 8ᵉ, ☎ 01–45–22–32–47, métro Havre-Caumartin; ⊠ 85 rue de Rennes, 6ᵉ, ☎ 01–42–22–61–49, métro Rennes; ⊠ 92 rue St-Antoine, 4ᵉ, ☎ 01–42–72–76–66, métro St-Paul; ⊠ 332 rue St-Honoré, 1ᵉʳ, ☎ 01–42–60–64–50, métro Tuileries) is chockablock with the sort of ingenious kitchen accoutrements that the French do so well, priced below what you would pay for such creativity back home.

Perfumes

Annick Goutal (⊠ 14 rue de Castiglione, 1ᵉʳ, ☎ 01–42–60–52–82, métro Concorde) sells this exclusive signature perfume line.

Guerlain (⊠ 68 av. des Champs-Elysées, 8ᵉ, ☎ 01–47–89–71–84, métro Franklin-D.-Roosevelt; ⊠ 47 rue Bonaparte, 6ᵉ, ☎ 01–43–26–71–19, métro Mabillon) boutiques are the only authorized Paris outlets for legendary perfumes like Shalimar, Chamade, and the latest, Champs-Elysées.

Shoes

Stéphane Kélian (⊠ 23 bd. de la Madeleine, 1ᵉʳ, ☎ 01–42–96–01–84, métro Madeleine; ⊠ 6 pl. des Victoires, 2ᵉ, ☎ 01–42–61–60–74, métro Bourse) creates chic, high-style, comfortable shoes for men and women.

Shopping Arcades

Paris's 19th-century commercial arcades, called *passages,* are the forerunners of the modern shopping mall. Glass roofs, decorative pillars, and inlaid mosaic floors make these spaces charming. Shops range from the avant-garde (Gaultier and Yukii Tori designs in the luxurious Galerie Vivienne) to the genteel (embroidery supplies and satin ribbons at Le Bonheur des Dames in the Passage Jouffroy). The major arcades are in the 1er and 2e arrondissements on the Right Bank.

Galerie Vivienne (⊠ 4 rue des Petits-Champs, 2e, métro Bourse), between the Stock Exchange (Bourse) and the Palais-Royal, is home to a range of interesting shops, an excellent tearoom, and Cave Legrand, a quality wine shop. **Passage Jouffroy** (⊠ 12 bd. Montmartre, 9e, métro Montmartre) is full of shops selling toys, postcards, antique canes, perfumes, original cosmetics, and dried flowers: Try Pain d'Epices (⊠ No. 29) and Au Bonheur des Dames (⊠ No. 39).

Markets

Le Marché aux Puces St-Ouen (métro Porte de Clignancourt), on Paris's northern boundary still attracts the crowds when it opens on weekends and Monday, but its once unbeatable prices are now a feature of the past. This century-old labyrinth of alleyways packed with antiques dealers' booths and junk stalls spreads for over a square mile. The clothing is downscale, but there are excellent finds in the bins of old prints and vintage advertisements. But be warned—if there's one place in Paris where you need to know how to bargain, this is it!

INDEX

X = *restaurant*, 🏨 = *hotel*

NOTES

NOTES

NOTES

Fodor's Travel Publications

Available at bookstores everywhere, or call 1–800–533–6478, 24 hours a day.

Gold Guides

U.S.

Alaska

Arizona

Boston

California

Cape Cod, Martha's
Vineyard, Nantucket

The Carolinas &
Georgia

Chicago

Colorado

Florida

Hawai'i

Las Vegas,
Reno, Tahoe

Los Angeles

Maine, Vermont,
New Hampshire

Maui & Lāna'i

Miami & the Keys

New England

New Orleans

New York City

Pacific North Coast

Philadelphia &
the Pennsylvania
Dutch Country

The Rockies

San Diego

San Francisco

Santa Fe, Taos,
Albuquerque

Seattle & Vancouver

The South

U.S. & British
Virgin Islands

USA

Virginia & Maryland

Walt Disney World,
Universal Studios
and Orlando

Washington, D.C.

Foreign

Australia

Austria

The Bahamas

Belize & Guatemala

Bermuda

Canada

Cancún, Cozumel,
Yucatán Peninsula

Caribbean

China

Costa Rica

Cuba

The Czech Republic &
Slovakia

Eastern &
Central Europe

Europe

Florence, Tuscany
& Umbria

France

Germany

Great Britain

Greece

Hong Kong

India

Ireland

Israel

Italy

Japan

London

Madrid & Barcelona

Mexico

Montréal &
Québec City

Moscow, St.
Petersburg, Kiev

The Netherlands,
Belgium &
Luxembourg

New Zealand

Norway

Nova Scotia,
New Brunswick,
Prince Edward Island

Paris

Portugal

Provence &
the Riviera

Scandinavia

Scotland

Singapore

South Africa

South America

Southeast Asia

Spain

Sweden

Switzerland

Thailand

Toronto

Turkey

Vienna & the Danu
Valley

Special-Interest Guides

Adventures to Imagine

Alaska Ports of Call

Ballpark Vacations

Caribbean Ports
of Call

The Complete Guide
to America's
National Parks

Disney Like a Pro

Europe Ports of Call

Family Adventures

Fodor's Gay Guide
to the USA

Fodor's How to Pack

Great American
Learning Vacations

Great American
Sports & Adventure
Vacations

Great American
Vacations

Great American
Vacations for
Travelers with
Disabilities

Halliday's New
Orleans Food
Explorer

Healthy Escapes

Kodak Guide to
Shooting Great
Travel Pictures

National Parks and
Seashores of the East

National Parks of
the West

Nights to Imagine

Rock & Roll Traveler
Great Britain
and Ireland

Rock & Roll Traveler
USA

Sunday in
San Francisco

Walt Disney Worl
for Adults

Weekends in
New York

Wendy Perrin's
Secrets Every S
Traveler Should

Where Should V
Take the Kids?
California

Where Should \
Take the Kids?
Northeast

Worldwide Cru
and Ports of Ca

WHEREVER YOU TRAVEL, *H*ELP IS NEVER FAR AWAY.

From planning your trip to providing travel assistance along the way, American Express® Travel Service Offices are always there to help you do more.

Paris

American Express Bureau de Change
14 Bd. de la Madeleine
1/53 30 50 94

American Express Bureau de Change
26 Avenue de L'Opéra
1/53 29 40 39

American Express TFS Bureau de Change
5 rue St. Eleuthère
1/42 23 93 52

American Express Travel Service
11 rue Scribe
1/47 77 77 07

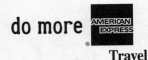

do more AMERICAN EXPRESS

Travel

http://www.americanexpress.com/travel

American Express Travel Service Offices are located throughout France.

In case you want to see the world.
At American Express, we're here to make your journey a smooth one. So we have over 1,700 travel service locations in over 120 countries ready to help. What else would you expect from the world's largest travel agency?
do more
AMERICAN EXPRESS
Travel
http://www.americanexpress.com/travel

In case you want to be welcomed there.

We're here to see that you're always welcomed at establishments everywhere. That's why millions of people carry the American Express® Card – for peace of mind, confidence, and security, around the world or just around the corner.

do more ®

AMERICAN
EXPRESS

Cards